BECOME
YOU

I highly recommend Nathanael White's new book, *Become You*. This is an amazing book that shows the reader the value of connecting with who God has created them to be. It's a powerful look at the power of identity that can only come from the Father. I recommend this book for church leaders as well, to empower them to lead through the power of identity!

—Luke Holter, speaker and award-winning author

I was blown away by the wisdom in this book. I felt a palpable importance of this transformational message with each turning page. I was compelled by the depth and gravity of the topic, and yet Nathanael so gently unwrapped it in such a way that it was easy to read and digest. This book reignited my gratitude that I am a loved son of the Most High God, made in his image! Once we know this, it has serious implications. It is from the outpouring of the Father's all-encompassing love that families and cultures are transformed. Once we understand our identity in that love—as Nathanael puts it, "I was born to be like God"—then and only then can we believe in and cheer each other on!

Furthermore, I have been on the receiving end of being looked square in the face by Nathanael White and having him say, "I believe in you." The author of this book not only has tremendous wisdom and revelation, but he actually lives out the truth of the kingdom he has learned, and I am a benefactor of that grace. I wholeheartedly recommend this life-changing book as well as the dynamic author by whom it was written.

—Jonathan Claussen MD, founder and president,
The Family Restoration Project

Become You will simply step you into defining your identity in God. It will open the door to what it really means to be a child of God and to truly walk in that title. I believe it will change the face of the church today and redefine many generations.

—Todd "Papabear" Finney, founder,
Papabear Preach & The Sojourners

Become You is giving me a newfound confidence to take risks and a newfound permission to fail, because, ultimately, God already sees me as a success. It's giving me fresh eyes with which to look upon our heavenly Father, his people, and myself.

—David Olson, senior pastor, SkyWater Church

Nathanael White—a man truly poised, instrumental, and being used mightily by God in these last days. He brings fresh *rhema*, helping individuals realize their true identity in Christ. Once people can accurately see themselves as God sees them, they can move mountains. Honored to know Nathanael for many years now and to be to colaborers for his kingdom and for his glory!

—Dave Wagner, co-founder and director, First Love MN

Are you looking for answers to questions about life with God that just don't seem to make sense? Nathanael effectively clarifies how life with God can be real, powerful, joyful, and truthful.

—Kristi Graner, founding pastor and director, Dare To Believe Ministries

This revolutionary book challenges each of us to reexamine our views of God, ourselves and each other. Nathanael probes beneath the surface of traditional thinking and unearths new insights and freedom to "Becoming You." The book is an adventure and journey drawing each of us into a deeper understanding of our splendid uniqueness and purpose. I emerged strengthened and resolved to fulfill the incredible blueprint God designed for my life.

—Diane Kucala, founder and chief leadership officer, Blueprint Leadership

The message God gave Nathanael, and is giving this generation of believers, is the one that will win the world. God really loves us as his children and is good to us always. He thinks we are wonderful! Nathanael uses beautiful analogies filled with depth of revelation as pictures of our preciousness to God. Knowing who we are and walking in a loving relationship with our heavenly Father causes us to walk as few Christians have. Nathanael clearly describes how God loves giving us his view of people while at the same time giving us the insight to be who we are: saints not sinners, sons and daughters not slaves. I was drawn over and over again into a deeper awareness of God's love for me.

—Rod Marquette, senior pastor, Destiny Church

Become You is a paradigm-altering work that will unveil your eyes to truly see and express the unique glory of God that only YOU can shine forth to the world around you! It draws you into a fresh and freeing biblical paradigm of who God is and who you are, and it lays a foundation of hope and freedom for you to envision yourself and your future. You will see yourself, the Lord, and the world around you differently after reading this book!

Reading this book is like drinking water and realizing it was quenching a thirst you didn't even know you had. In these pages Nathanael White gives a foundation, language, and context to the concept of identity that will surely reshape the way you see the Lord and his mandate to you to express his image on the earth.

Become You is a fresh breath of God that will awaken your spirit from the inside out. These pages will take you on a journey to discover not only who you were created to be but also the heart of the loving, trusting, and empowering Father who created you to rule and reign with him.

—Kristen D'Arpa, staff member at The House Church and founder of Go Glocal Ministries

BECOME YOU

Discover the **mindsets** that lead to your **powerful, unique identity**

NATHANAEL WHITE

BECOME YOU: Discover the Mind-Sets that Lead to Your Powerful, Unique Indentity

© Copyright 2016 Nathanael White

ISBN 978-0-9981508-0-2

All rights reserved. This book is protected by the copyright laws of the United States of America. This book may not be copied or reprinted for commercial gain or profit. The use of short quotations or occasional page copying for personal or group study is permitted and encouraged. Permission will be granted upon request.

Unless otherwise indicated, all Scripture quotations are from the ESV® Bible (The Holy Bible, English Standard Version®), copyright © 2001 by Crossway, a publishing ministry of Good News Publishers. Used by permission. All rights reserved. All emphasis within Scripture quotations is the author's own.

I dedicate this book, first, to my parents, who raised me to love the Lord and his Word, and who encouraged a life of courageous wonder to explore the mysteries of God. Without this foundation I never would have discovered the truths in this book.

Second, I dedicate this book to my children and their children unto generations I will never meet in this world. May these truths be your foundation. I cannot even begin to imagine what you will accomplish when what I have written becomes so foundational that it is elementary. As I am building on my parents' foundation, may you build on mine many times over.

CONTENTS

Acknowledgments xiii

Foreword xv

Introduction xix

SECTION ONE: THE BLUEPRINT

Chapter 1   Why Were You Born? 3

Every generation in the history of the world has worked to discover why we exist. Interestingly, God revealed the answer before he even created us. It is only when we learn this not-so-hidden truth that we can begin to live as God intended—powerful, free, fulfilled, and confident in who we are.

Chapter 2   The Truth about Glory 17

Generations of Christians have declared that we exist for God's glory. This is true, but what if one small shift in perspective could change what this means and how we think about who God is toward us? In reality, God's nature demands him to be focused on us. Far from making us prideful, this revelation is actually the key we need to help us follow God's plan to make us like him.

Chapter 3   Who Says? 35

Many voices speak to us every day, trying to convince us to follow them. Most of those voices tell us how terrible we are, continually tearing us down to keep us from becoming who God made us to be. The key to our destiny, then, is to learn what God says about us and cling to his voice relentlessly. There is only one voice that matters—our Father's.

Chapter 4   Sons, Not Sinners 45

One thing keeps Christians trapped in failure more than anything else, and it's all one big lie. This lie convinces God's children they are still enslaved to sin to such an extent that they embrace it as their identity, calling themselves sinners. The truth of God's Word, however, gives us a new name and a new identity as new creations. This new life returns us to God's intent—that we would be made in his image.

Chapter 5   Becoming like God 59

Many words can be used to describe God—righteous, holy, creator, etc.—but one word rises above all the others to describe his personhood—love. It is as we remain in his love that we enter the process of becoming like him, and if we become like him, it won't be long until love is not just a word that describes God. Soon it will also describe us.

Chapter 6   Divine Contradiction. 73

You can't become who God made you to be without loving yourself. But you also can't become who God made you to be without serving others' dreams before your own. While these two truths may seem to contradict each other, learning to walk the balance between them is one of the most important lessons we need to learn in order to become ourselves.

Chapter 7   The Tree of Death 89

Christians make long lists of rules they think they must live by, but this isn't the kind of life God intended for us. Looking through history, we discover that rules were never really very important to God and we learn when and why he made rules at all. Ultimately, we discover that rules lead to independence from God and death, a hopeless life in which we need God to save us not just from death, but from the rules that brought it in the first place.

Chapter 8   The Tree of Life. 105

God never intended Christians to live by rules, but instead for us to live by the Holy Spirit until we become like him. In this life, God's identity is the standard for our living, wisdom teaches us how to live, and the process of becoming like God starts by simply becoming his child.

SECTION TWO: THE PROCESS

Chapter 9   Permission to Change 125

Becoming like God means we have to change. Change means we need to count the cost of leaving the life we are used to. But change also means embracing a life so incredible that it can only be described as being like God. In this new life, we are no longer concerned with the past, but instead with our amazing future with Jesus.

Chapter 10   The Power of Your Voice. 141

As we discover who God made us to be, we also need to discover the tools he created to help us live our unique identity. Hands down, the most powerful tool he gives us is our voice. Knowing how powerful our voice is, where our voice comes from, and how to shape our words sets us on a straight path toward our incredible purpose.

Chapter 11   Deep Roots 155

When God speaks his promise over our lives, it almost always feels urgent. We sense that his promise could happen at any moment! The reality, however, is that time is often the most important ingredient to our identity. We can't arrive overnight, but waiting is worth it. Articulating a clear vision is the key to sustaining our faith as we wait for God's promises.

SECTION THREE: BE FREE

Chapter 12   Created to Rule 171

The image of God is who we were created to be, but what were we created to do? God's original declaration over humankind unleashed a powerful statement about our purpose. Giving us room to dream with God about the life we can have in him, this statement is strong, free, important, and good. It is God's declaration that we were created to rule!

Chapter 13   God Follows You 185

When we first believe in Jesus, we have to follow him for a time to learn how to live as he does. His process teaches us his heart, and once we know his heart, he begins to empower us to make our own decisions. His goal is not that we would follow him our entire life, but that we would grow to a point where he begins to follow us.

Notes 197

ACKNOWLEDGMENTS

Amy—you always believe in me. Thanks for being my sounding board, for your patience and faithfulness, and for your daring in taking this life journey with me.

Mom and Dad—for the immeasurable gift you have given me in our common faith. Thank you for showing me a life that truly pursues Jesus.

Jamey and Nikki—you taught me how to hear God's voice and stand in who God made me to be. I'm forever in your debt.

Presence Church family—thank you for experimenting with me, for believing in me, and for believing in yourselves. Our lives are becoming the firstfruits of this book's message.

The House Church family, especially the elders—thank you for being a community that believes anything is possible, for cheering me on, and for encouraging me that people need to hear this book's message.

My children—you inspire me to reach for greatness and humble me with the practicalities of real life. Thank you for loving me so faithfully and consummately.

David Sluka and Rhonda Kalal—you are the reasons I write. Without your invitations, open doors, training, and impartations, none of this would have happened and my life would be entirely different. Thanks for being God's instruments to help direct my path.

My editorial team—I know full well that good books are never written alone. Thank you, Christy Distler, Christy Callahan, and Katherine Lloyd, for your skills in editing, proofreading, and design. You've helped take this book to the next level. Also, special thanks to *one designs* at 99designs.com for creating a cover I love.

ACKNOWLEDGMENTS

Deepest thanks to the Johnson family, Dan and Trish Notley, Jim and Carole Smith, Gary and Suzanne White, Dela White, Al and Julie D'Arpa, and an anonymous donor who all gave generously to my Kickstarter campaign. Without them, this book would not have been printed.

FOREWORD

There have been several awakenings during the last two thousand years of church history. Each one has resulted in that generation experiencing something of God that had not been experienced by the previous generation. Often God would point to an area of society or a specific truth within their belief system and bring about repentance. This change in mindset would cause the church of that day to suddenly experience a shift in how they lived life. Each awakening was marked by the masses turning to Jesus and persecution coming from the previous generation. Because each generation believed they understood a deep truth about God, when correction or adjustment came through the following generation, the sharp disagreement would produce conflict. Yet wisdom is always vindicated by her fruit. As God would bring increasing revelation, people would be transformed and the voices of distention would pass away.

The questions of *Who am I?* and *What am I here for?* are not new. The reason these questions continue to remain powerful is because of how important they are. It is essential to have them answered if you want your life to have significance. These questions cause each Christ follower to examine their life and search for their own personal authenticity. The combination of knowing who God has made you to be and what he has called you to do empowers a person to face adversity with confidence. It also provides power to overcome shortcomings and step into the greater calling of God.

Growing up in the church, I personally experienced the ramifications of people saying one thing on Sunday mornings and then their life

FOREWORD

not matching the rhetoric. My own experience with church was a great emphasis on the accuracy of doctrine, with little emphasis on manifesting the things so eloquently preached. I watched many in my generation turn away from the church because of this dichotomy. As the Lord breathes on his church, many of these same people have returned to follow Christ and rejoined the ranks of the church. They are carrying with them a great emphasis on the need to be authentic. The marriage of good doctrine and living it out have become a banner for my generation. There is a groundswell of believers who are working to see the things they read in the Bible become a reality in their lives.

I believe this is what paves the way for another awakening. One of the earmarks of what God is doing in our generation is the discovery of just how fearfully and wonderfully made we are. This understanding is producing followers of Jesus who see who God made them to be, and as a result they are living supernatural lives. Great works of God are happening worldwide. Whole people groups are coming to know Jesus, and nations are being discipled in the ways of the kingdom. These great works are being done by normal, everyday believers. They gather in churches on the weekends for worship and then demonstrate heaven as they go about their daily lives.

The authentic expression of who God made you to be is foundational to living a life of fulfillment. This book covers topics that are essential in understanding your purpose and discovering your true identity in Christ Jesus. I have personally known and walked alongside Nathanael White for over ten years of ministry and have seen how this message has shaped his life. He embodies the truths presented here and lives a life that demonstrates Jesus. Nathanael is a pastor and an elder in the church I personally lead. He is both trusted and trustworthy. And his book covers topics that are essential to understanding your purpose and discovering your true identity in Christ Jesus. These are not just ideas, but principles lived out and demonstrated. I am so excited that he took time to write these things down so others can experience the awesome fruit they bring!

The pursuit of being deeply rooted in Jesus is central to becoming

FOREWORD

who God made you to be. Christ in you is truly the hope of glory. My prayer is that this book will cause you to dive deep into the reality that God lives inside you, and that you would grow in your trust of his voice as he shapes and guides your life. There have been many awakenings in church history; perhaps the one that will mark this generation will come forth as you "Become You."

JAMEY VANGELDER, Senior Leader,
The House Church, www.ithehouse.org

INTRODUCTION

A number of years ago, a beautiful sunrise drew me upstairs in my townhome to the place where I could get the best view. There, from my daughter's bedroom, I watched the unfolding of one of the most beautiful things I have ever seen.

The strange part about it was that it happened on a completely overcast day. I couldn't see any sky, only clouds, and normally that would mean there could be no beautiful sunrise. Somehow, though, on this day there must have been just enough of a crack near the horizon for the sun to shine its beautiful rays underneath the canopy of clouds.

This all worked together to paint the sky from top to bottom and front to back with the largest and most brilliant sunrise imaginable, aflame with the reds, pinks, and oranges of the sun. Not a single speck of gray remained in the clouds as the entire sky became gloriously illuminated. As I soaked it all in, I heard God say to me, "This is what my church looks like."

Like so many times when God speaks to me, his words caused an explosion of thoughts in my mind so that I understood the depths of what he was saying. It all started with a passage from the book of Revelation that I had been reading. Near the end of it, an angel comes to the apostle John and says, "Come, I will show you the Bride, the wife of the Lamb" (Revelation 21:9).

The angel carries John away in the Spirit to an enormous mountain, where he sees a city descending from heaven, shining with the glory of God. He describes this city, saying that the foundations are layer upon layer of precious stones, twelve layers in all, with each one a different kind of stone including all the colors of the rainbow. The walls built on the foundations are made of precious stone as well.

INTRODUCTION

Within the city are streets of such pure gold that John twice calls them transparent, clear as crystal. At the very center of the city is God himself, shining to provide this city with its light.

Now, explaining this here took some time, but when God said to me, "This is what my church looks like," everything came together in just seconds, twisting my brain this way and that as I tried to grasp it all. Immediately I understood that I needed to pay attention to what the angel told John before he saw this city—that this picture is not of the city where the Bride will live, but it is a picture of the Bride herself. It's a prophetic, metaphorical picture like the beasts Daniel saw that represented kingdoms (Daniel 7). John saw a city that represented something else, and the angel interpreted the vision for us to tell us what the city represents. The city is the church, the Bride of Christ Jesus.

This made more sense when I considered 1 Peter 2:5, which says, "You yourselves like living stones are being built up as a spiritual house." That's when I understood that the "living stones" Peter compares us to are not granite or brick but the precious stones John saw when God revealed to him the completed house, entirely made of gems and jewels!

Again, this is all metaphorical language. Of course, I'm not saying that anyone in the church is literally a precious stone. I'm saying that this is the language from Scripture that God uses to describe us, which means that we can look at these pictures to understand how God thinks of us, and, from that, learn to think of ourselves the same way.

HOW GOD SEES YOU

The final layer of this revelation that came as I watched the sunrise had to do with you. God brought the two pictures together for me—the sunrise with the picture of the Bride in Revelation. He said, "If you took a digital picture of this sunrise and zoomed in on it until you could see every individual pixel, each pixel is like one precious stone in the wall of that city, and each precious stone is one believer in my Church."

Now the picture was finally coming together. You are a precious

INTRODUCTION

stone, and so am I, and so is everyone who believes in Jesus to become part of his Bride. But each of us is a different kind of precious stone, and just as I was taught once upon a time when shopping for engagement rings, each stone has its own cut, color, clarity, and carat (weight), making each stone perfectly unique. More than that, every cut is made to maximize the color and clarity and how they work together with light so that each stone reaches its most beautiful potential. The picture we see is a city made of you and me, precious stones of differing colors, layer upon layer, each one cut and designed to display the greatest beauty.

What comes next is the most amazing part, because the light that shines on us isn't man-made light in a jeweler's display case or even sunlight. It's the light of God himself! What effect would his light potentially have on the splendor of this incredible scene as each precious stone becomes a prism to refract his glory into an array of colors such as has never been seen before!

That's when I understood what God was telling me through that sunrise. He showed me the big picture that what John saw was the church shining with God's own glory radiating from within her, creating a masterpiece that must have been like a three-dimensional rainbow that filled the sky with magnificent luminosity from horizon to horizon.

And he showed me the micropicture, the truth that every single one of us is part of this picture. Every single one of us is a pixel in the sunrise and a precious stone in the city. Each of us is unique. Each of us is necessary. And each of us is indescribably beautiful.

I'll let that sink in for a moment, because, yes, I'm talking about you and me.

This is the vision that, more than anything else, ignited a passion within me to see all people become who God created them to be. I realized that your identity is the cut, color, clarity, and carat of your precious stone. That's how you interpret the metaphor. If something is lacking from your identity, if something can degrade you to keep you from becoming the fullness of what God made you to be, then it means one of those precious stones was left raw and uncut. It's untapped, leaving so much

INTRODUCTION

potential beauty inside and unrevealed, hiding not just the magnificence of who you are but also the indescribable beauty of God that he created you to display.

I BELIEVE IN YOU

Not long ago, I was sitting with a friend at a conference. Life wasn't going well for him at the time, and it would have been putting it mildly to say that he could have been doing better. The worship team was leading everyone else in song as God's presence filled the room in wave after wave, but I knew that for this moment the most important thing for me to do was to take care of my friend.

I put my arm around him and said, "Hey, I know things aren't good right now, but I want you to know something. I believe in you, and I will keep believing in you until you believe in yourself again."

He tearfully thanked me, my words obviously hitting home. I returned to my seat in the front row and reflected on what had just happened. Suddenly, it was like a movie was playing in my mind, a vision of myself later that day when I was going to announce an identity class that I was going to teach. I saw myself standing at the podium, looking intently out over the crowd and heard myself passionately telling them, "I believe in you!"

These words resonated loudly in my spirit. I asked God what he was trying to tell me, saying, "God, I know you believe in me. You've been teaching me that for years."

He said, "I know, son, but I'm showing you your life's message. Your life's message is, 'I believe in you.'"

Now I started tearing up. I knew that God had taken me on a journey of identity for nine solid years to help me understand who I am and how to help others take the same journey. What I hadn't realized was how this message of "I believe in you" had been part of my life for much longer, ever since I'd given my life to Jesus. Through my mind passed countless friends and relationships where that phrase defined the basis of our relationship—I believe in you, and I'll keep believing in you until you believe

INTRODUCTION

in yourself again. I had lived this unknowingly time after time after time for more than half my life.

This is my message to you from the very beginning of this book: I believe in you. It doesn't matter to me whether you believe in yourself yet or not; I still believe in you. More importantly, I know God believes in you.

I know this with absolute certainty because I have seen the vision of the precious stone he created you to be—someone unique, beautiful in character and personhood, and mysteriously powerful who has an ability to display God's glory to the world in a way no other human being in history can.

I know that no matter what the world has said, no matter what religion has said, I need you and so does the rest of this world. I know that you are not just important; you are essential. I know that if you can just discover with confidence who God made you to be, you'll love being you—and when you just be yourself, it will absolutely transform the world around you.

I know this, because that's who you are. That's why I believe in you. I always have and I always will.

WHERE WE'RE GOING

You might feel a little self-conscious and think what I'm saying is a little over the top. That's okay. But I know as you read through these pages, you'll see God in a way that helps you understand why I'm so forward about this.

God is absolutely wild about you. He really is. And what you'll find as you read this book is that first I'll go through a number of mindsets about God and ourselves that are necessary for us to have if we're going to become all God made us to be. I call this section The Blueprint.

Second, you'll read a few chapters that lay out practical details for how to actually begin putting those mindsets to practice and use in daily life. I call this section The Process.

Finally, you'll find the last section where I'll encourage you to begin

BECOME YOU

dreaming with God. Whereas The Blueprint section is very big-picture and covers everyone, this final section is where the focus gets much more individualized. I call this last section Be Free.

When it's all done, my prayer for you is that you'll be well on your way to being connected with God in a way that transforms you day by day, month by month, and year by year, more and more into everything you were born to be, releasing you into a life that is beautiful, fulfilling, powerful, and free. My prayer is that God would cause his presence to rest on my words so they become his instrument to shape you into that precious stone I saw all those years ago—flawless, magnificent, radiant, and filled with his glory.

Unto that end, let's do this together. I believe in you!

Nathanael White

[Handwritten note:]
The Blueprint
The Process
Be Free

BECOME YOU

SECTION ONE
THE BLUEPRINT

Chapter 1

WHY WERE YOU BORN?

Every generation in the history of the world has worked to discover why we exist. Interestingly, God revealed the answer before he even created us. It is only when we learn this not-so-hidden truth that we can begin to live as God intended—powerful, free, fulfilled, and confident in who we are.

It all started in a garden. Well, at least that's as far back as any human can remember. The first memory any of us had was waking up in paradise with God our Father kneeling next to us, having just breathed into us our first breath of life.

Life in the garden of Eden was beautiful. In many ways it was the most beautiful the world has yet seen. Everything was perfect. Everything was good. Best of all, God was there with the first man and woman, sharing unbroken relationship with them as they walked together in the cool of the day. How could it have gotten any better?

But as good as things were, the world was raw, and so were our first father and mother. Just as C. S. Lewis wrote in another creation story, Adam and Eve could have said, "We are awake. We love. We think. We speak. We know … But please, we don't know very much yet."[1] That's exactly how everything that was so good was lost so quickly.

Adam and Eve weren't in the garden of Eden for very long before trouble came knocking at their proverbial door. You probably already know the bottom line of what happened. Satan came to Eve disguised as a crafty serpent and tempted her to eat the one fruit God had forbidden. She caved to the pressure, ate the fruit, and gave it to Adam who also ate. Just like that, the world fell into sin.

Nothing has been the same since that day. But stop right there. Most Christians know this story well. They know all about *sin*. It's what frames their understanding of their history, God's plan for salvation, and the world around them. Sin defines much about what is meaningful to them in this story of our origin.

But what if there's something more for us to see? What if there's something in this story that gives us the key we need to discover a life even more beautiful than the one in the garden? What if we could look beyond humankind's fall to see God's purpose for creating humankind in the first place? And what if that discovery had the power to take away the nasty, shameful feeling we all have experienced because of that word, *sin*?

Incredibly, the truth God spoke before he even made us will do all that and more in our lives. The truth I'm talking about comes from the very first thing God says about humankind.

THE INTENT OF GOD'S HEART

First impressions are important. This can be true even when you read the Bible. Oftentimes as you read, the first time something is mentioned is the most important time you'll read about it in the Bible. This is called the Principle of First Mention, and it basically says that whatever you learn about something the first time it is mentioned, that lesson should color everything else you learn about it from that point forward.

We find the first thing God ever said about humankind in Genesis 1:26: "And God said, 'Let us make man in our image, after our likeness.'"

These are powerful words, and they become even more powerful when we remember the context in which they are written. Genesis 1 is the narrative of how God created the world. Each day begins by God speaking, and once he has spoken, something brand-new bursts into existence. Sit on that one for a moment—every time God spoke, it happened exactly as he said it. Nothing deviated from what he spoke.

That's the context where it says, "And God said ..." Everything God said exploded into reality, and then God said something again! But this time what he said had nothing to do with the universe or the world around us. This time he spoke intimate words about you and me. He spoke the very heartbeat and purpose for why he made us. He revealed the dream in his heart that inspired him to birth creation in the first place: "Let us make man in our image, after our likeness."

This is who we were made to be. A lot of theologians and philosophers throughout history have labored to discover why humankind exists, but how often is it that the hardest things to find are hiding right in the open the whole time?

I believe that's what has happened here. I believe this is a truth God spoke from the very foundation of the world, creating a DNA of purpose for us that existed before he shaped a single strand of our physical makeup. This DNA of purpose produces within us a cry, asking, "Why am I alive? Why was I born?" It permeates every culture, every race, every religion, and every philosophy. It is foundational to our existence.

And of course it is, because God spoke it, and so it was created just as he said it.

GOD'S INVITATION

God made us to be like him. Because this is the first thing he—let alone anyone else—ever said about us, it needs to shape and color everything else we know about ourselves. Let me spell this out a little.

God said. The fact that our identity is founded in being like God is established by no less an authority than God himself. I can't stress this

BECOME YOU

enough. God himself is the one who said these words. He is the one with the authority and power to create simply by speaking and then to uphold his creation by the power of his word. Creation itself owes its existence to the power of his sustaining voice still echoing the declaration that caused the world to be. This voice also continues to whisper to our souls who we are and why he made us, and calls to us to remember those words he spoke before he shaped us, that we are made to be like him.

Imagine your life if this voice became the loudest voice you heard. What would your life be like if the voice that declares, "I was born to be like God" drowned out all the other voices that seek to shout us down to insignificance? What if the voices of "I'm fat and ugly," "I'm sinful," and, "I'm ashamed of myself" were silenced by the voice of confidence that God's overarching goal for your life is to make you like him?

What if it didn't matter what terrible thing your father, mother, siblings, friends, second grade teacher, or high school coach said about you? What if those words could be erased by more powerful words that were spoken about you long before anyone could try to tear you down?

How would you live if you didn't feel any pressure to perform a certain way? What if you could remove all those expectations that swirl around us and just live as who you were made to be? Can you imagine that life?

That is the life God invites you to. In fact, the reason people experience dissatisfaction with the life they have is because they don't have this life—the life of a person made in God's image.

THE CORE OF EVERY ISSUE

Adam and Eve were created with this life, but from the beginning Satan has attacked this life to try to keep us from living it. He hates that God made us to be like him, because that is what Satan wanted for himself. Isaiah 14:14 tells us that Satan said to himself, "I will ascend above the heights of the clouds; I will make myself like the Most High."

That was Satan's desire, but it wasn't why God made him, so it was a position not right for him to pursue. When he set himself to be like God, he was thrown down, transformed from Lucifer the archangel to Satan the twisting serpent. Imagine his wrath when he heard God say, "Let us make man in our image, after our likeness." The very thing he desired that was kept from him, God gave freely to humankind.

So he hated Adam and Eve, and he hates all of us who descend from them because we have what he wants yet cannot have. He works continually to keep us from living up to our created purpose, to deceive us into cutting ourselves short of it.

He started right away with Eve, and his words to her are telling. This is how it happened:

> Now the serpent was more crafty than any other beast of the field that the LORD God had made. He said to the woman, "Did God actually say, 'You shall not eat of any tree in the garden'?" And the woman said to the serpent, "We may eat of the fruit of the trees in the garden, but God said, 'You shall not eat of the fruit of the tree that is in the midst of the garden, neither shall you touch it, lest you die.'" But the serpent said to the woman, "You will not surely die. *For God knows that when you eat of it your eyes will be opened, and you will be like God*, knowing good and evil." —Genesis 3:1–5

Satan begins in a way that seems innocent enough. He just asks a question. It flatters Eve and plays to her commission to have dominion over "every creeping thing that creeps on the earth" (Genesis 1:26). It seems that he places himself beneath her instruction, learning what the boundaries are for the garden.

Before long, however, he asserts himself, offering his own deceptive opinion of the situation. Like before, he plays toward what God already said, but this time his words trick Eve: "If you eat this fruit, *then* you will be like God!" (my paraphrase). He strikes directly at God's very heart and intent in making Adam and Eve, promising a shortcut to its fulfillment in their lives while simultaneously accusing God of holding out on them.

This is the core deception that has plagued humankind ever since—that we have to labor in our own strength to accomplish what God promised for us before we were even made.

I have five children, and four of them are boys. Every one of them, when they were young, thought they were as big and as strong as I am. They believe they can run as fast, jump as high, outwrestle, outmuscle, and outwork their old man. They were and are blissfully ignorant, and thankfully so. They are children.

While I know they haven't matured into the fullness of my image as chips off the old block, they think they're just like me. No one could convince them otherwise. But someone might be able to convince them to try a shortcut. Why not? They're innocent. They trust most people and have good reason to because no one has taken advantage of them.

The thing is, no shortcut could ever help them. Only two things will help them grow to become like me—deep relationship and time. But they don't even know what time is yet. When I asked my four-year-old what he thought about a twelve-day trip I took to Africa, he said, "I thought you were gone for LOTS of YEARS!"

I think Eve had this kind of childlike ignorance. She knew the goal was to be like God, so if this fruit could help her do that without leading to anything bad, then why not? Adam knew he was doing something wrong, yet together they went for the shortcut. Satan tricked them into working for something God had already given and promised them.

At the heart of Satan's deception is the idea of lack. You see, Eve was already made to be like God. Sure, she probably wasn't living in the fullness of it yet, but she didn't need to eat the fruit to make it happen. If she had just looked around her, she would've seen that the whole world she lived in screamed God's goodness to her, how he labored to prepare a wonderful home for humankind.

There was a purpose to everything he spoke into being. Every stroke of his creative brush made something that laid a foundation for humankind's home and furnished it with decorations so lavish that parts of humankind still worship them to this day. Each step of creation both beautified and served a purpose, all building toward there being a perfect garden, inside the perfect land of Eden, inside a perfect world, inside a perfect universe, created by a perfect God. God painted a target at which to aim his affections and then placed humankind in the bull's-eye.

God prepared a world with every resource Adam and Eve could ever possibly need for life, beauty, or purpose and then walked with them in that place every day. They knew his voice and his presence. They even knew his touch. They needed nothing, yet somehow in that moment they felt lack. Satan first convinced them of it, and then he convinced them to labor on their own to make up for it. When they took the bait, that's when they fell.

THE TACTIC NEVER CHANGES

If we fast-forward several thousand years, we see that Satan used the exact same tactic with Jesus in Matthew 4:1–11. Our Savior had been in the wilderness for forty days and had become extremely hungry. At Jesus' weakest point, Satan came to tempt him.

Two times Satan challenged him, "If you're the Son of God ..." Change stones to bread. Jump off the temple. Prove you are who God says you are. Show you have no lack. It was the same thing he did to Adam and Eve. They were made to be like God, and Satan tore them down as lacking what God promised, as falling short of who God made them to be. Jesus was born the Son of God, and Satan tried to tear him down as lacking what God promised, daring him to prove he was who God made him to be. Twice Satan challenged him and twice Jesus shut him down, choosing to rest in his Father's work and timing in his life.

So Satan launched a third attack, tempting Jesus to take the shortcut. He knew Jesus was destined to be king over the whole world, yet he also knew he had authority to offer that to Jesus without the suffering of the cross. Satan did offer this to Jesus, saying, "All these [kingdoms of the world] I will give you, if you will fall down and worship me" (Matthew 4:9). Again, Jesus refused. He kept faith that his Father was good and would never withhold what he promised, that he would cause Jesus to become who he was born to be.

Where Adam and Eve fell short, Jesus held firm. He showed us the victory that comes when we simply remember, sometimes stubbornly through adversity, who God says we are.

STORIES OF VICTORY

Jesus isn't the only scriptural example of people who gained victory because they clung to the identity God gave them.

We can start with David, who wandered into the camp of Israel's army to deliver food to his brothers. David had no reason to have confidence in who he was. He was born from what was assumed to be an adulterous relationship (later vindicated), was the youngest in his family, and had always been treated as an outcast. More than that, he had enough Gentile blood in him from his Moabite great-grandmother that even his father questioned their family's legitimacy as true Israelites.

Yet David was the only one who heard the taunts of the giant Goliath and responded, "Who is this uncircumcised Philistine, that he should defy the armies of the living God?" (1 Samuel 17:26). David knew who he was—an Israelite who belonged to the living God—and because he knew who he was, he knew no man could mock him and get away with it. (Goliath didn't get away with it. He got a rocketing stone in his forehead that knocked him out so David could steal his sword to cut off his head.)

Elijah also knew who he was. After telling King Ahab that it wouldn't rain until he said so, he prayed fervently for three years and it didn't rain. Bringing a climax to his challenge, Elijah called the prophets of Baal to a showdown on Mount Carmel—whoever's god answered their prayers with fire from heaven was the true God.

After the prophets of Baal yelled, screamed, danced, cut themselves, and lathered all day long, working to get a spark and getting nothing, Elijah stepped forward. He prayed, "O LORD … let it be known this day that you are God in Israel, *and that I am your servant*, and that I have done all these things at your word" (1 Kings 18:36). Immediately, fire fell from heaven so powerfully that it even consumed the stones on which the sacrifice had been set.

While these two stories feature men who seem to have always known who they were, countless other stories tell of men and women who had questions when they encountered God but were changed because of that encounter. Gideon said, "I'm the least of the least," but God said he was a man of valor. Isaiah said, "Woe is me! I'm a man of unclean lips!" But God sent him as a prophet to many nations and chose him to give some of the most intimate prophecies about Jesus. Jeremiah said, "I'm too young," but God said, "I will use you to establish nations and to tear nations down." And Sarah said, "I'm barren," but God said her son would give her laughter again.

This even is true of when the Pharisees wondered about the disciples, "How did these men learn to speak? Aren't they from Galilee?" Then they realized, "They must have been with Jesus," because even they knew the effect Jesus had on people's lives.

Over and over again, countless men, women, judges, prophets, and kings defined their lives by their lack until they met God and he declared his word over their lives. Each time God spoke over them the identity he created for them, it brought them to victory and destiny.

THE SAME IS TRUE FOR US

While we like to think of our culture today as more advanced and sophisticated than the historic societies of Bible times, people are actually pretty much the same. It's in our DNA from our first father and mother.

Adam and Eve couldn't have known even the beginnings of the incredible responsibility they had, making a choice that would affect every human being in such a profound way. Nevertheless, that is the responsibility—and the opportunity—they had. Adam bore this responsibility in particular, as the apostle Paul makes clear in Romans 5:12: "Therefore, just as sin came into the world through one man, and death through sin, and so death spread to all men because all sinned." In other words, Adam was the gateway to all humankind. He let sin in and it has wreaked havoc among us ever since.

Adam and Eve chose to work to provide for themselves apart from God what God had already promised to give them through relationship. As soon as they did, they fell into sin. The first result of this was shame.

Immediately their eyes were opened, they recognized they were naked, and they ran for cover to hide themselves. In the life they had before sin, they were free. They could live in perfect relationship with God, each other, themselves, and the world around them, but as soon as shame entered their hearts, all of that was broken. They no longer had any perfect relationship, least of all with themselves, because the first thing shame says in your mind is, "Look at all these things that are wrong with you!" The most natural response to that voice is to reduce yourself to what you perceive to be the most acceptable version of you and desperately hide everything else, even from yourself.

Just as Adam opened the gateway of humanity to sin so that all have sinned, in that same moment he also universally opened our gateway to shame. Researcher Brené Brown has spent years researching shame, and one of her most profound discoveries is that shame is a nearly universal human experience. The only people who do not experience shame are psychopaths.[2]

The rest of us all experience shame. We might as well talk about it, because addressing it is the only way out of it. Thankfully, God has provided a way out of all forms of shame, which I will talk about in a later chapter, but it's important to introduce the subject here so we can begin to see ourselves more clearly in the shoes of those biblical heroes who began ashamed but became transformed by encountering God.

The first step out of any problem is to clearly identify the problem. In this case, the problem is a sequence of events. It begins with a sense of lack. It continues with our stepping out to provide for ourselves apart from God what God has already promised to us. The result is sin, which leads to shame, which further isolates us from God because his radiance only reminds us of our darkness, so we hide. We try to present to him only the things that we have polished up as best we can, as though he doesn't know who we really are.

When we experience shame, what we perceive as negative about ourselves can become more prominent in our thoughts than what we perceive as good. Or, to put it a different way, our ashamed thoughts seem big while our confident thoughts are small. Our small thoughts about ourselves lead us to small actions.

How we see ourselves will always determine the influence we have on the world around us, either ushering in or limiting the victories we can have for God, ourselves, and the world. Think about the examples I gave earlier. David walked into a camp full of people who were powerless against Goliath, not because he was bigger than they were but because they felt small long before they laid eyes on the giant. The army felt small, but David felt big even though he was the smallest in the camp.

The same was true for the Israelites as they camped on the edge of the Promised Land. Ten spies returned to the nation, saying, "We're going to die! There are giants and we are like grasshoppers in their sight!" But two spies returned, saying, "We can do it! God has given us this land!" God confirmed to them what has been true for humankind throughout our history—that what they thought about themselves determined their future victory or failure. The ones who were convinced of failure went on to fail and die in the wilderness. The ones who were convinced of success went on to conquer the land.

GOD'S PURPOSE NEVER CHANGED

Of course, none of these heroes ever succeeded on their own or in their own strength. They won the day because God was with them, but that's the point from the beginning. God never desired for us to be separated from him; he desires for us become like him through relationship with him.

His desire has never changed. Remember that this was his stated purpose for creating us in the very beginning. It was the first statement ever made about humankind, and it was made by God himself. This truth colors everything else we talk about or do.

Recent movements within Christianity have rightfully placed a high emphasis on the gospel of salvation. They have studied the Bible to show how God's plan for salvation is woven through the entire story of Scripture. This is all very true and good, but as crazy as it might sound, I don't believe the gospel of salvation is the central point of the Bible. As important and essential as it is, I don't believe it's even the central point of God's relationship with humankind.

Here's why I think this: The gospel of salvation is God's plan for restoration, but we need to wonder what we are being restored to. I was taught that salvation restores us to relationship with God, and that is so unthinkably incredible as to defy all words or imagination. It's better than good and more than any of us could ask for. But God is so good that he offers more. He has a purpose in his relationship with us, a goal he stated for us before sin ever entered the picture.

He expressed a plan for humankind to make us like him before he expressed his plan to save us from sin. Sin didn't just damage our relationship with God and bring death; it also marred his image within us. But salvation restores us to a relationship with him so he can shape us in his image again. Consider these passages that describe how God works to make us like him:

> For those whom he foreknew he also predestined to be *conformed to the image of his Son*, in order that he might be the firstborn among many brothers.—Romans 8:29

> And we all, with unveiled face, beholding the glory of the Lord, *are being transformed into the same image* from one degree of glory to another.—2 Corinthians 3:18

> But that is not the way you learned Christ!—assuming that you have heard about him and were taught in him ... to be renewed

in the spirit of your minds, and *to put on the new self, created after the likeness of God* in true righteousness and holiness.—Ephesians 4:20–24

Do not lie to one another, seeing that you have put off the old self with its practices and have put on *the new self, which is being renewed in knowledge after the image of its creator.*—Colossians 3:9–10

Do you see how God's plan in saving us is to renew his image in us? Paul even directly says that this is the message we should learn when we learn Christ, that receiving him includes putting off our old self and putting on a brand-new us that is made in his image.

This is incredible news! It shows us how God's declared intent for humankind has never changed. Sin couldn't mar us beyond his repair, and Jesus' sacrifice accomplished more for us than simply the forgiveness of sins. It actually reversed the effect of sin so that what once caused us to fall away from God's likeness is now completely removed from us, replaced by God's very own Spirit, who works in us to make us like him again!

HOW DO YOU SEE GOD?

The question we need to answer, then, is how do you see God? Because how you see God will determine who you become. Three of the verses above clearly tell us that becoming like God is a process, not an instant transformation. Two of the verses specifically say it happens as we renew our minds or our knowledge.

What this means is that the gap between you now and you fully conformed to God's image is what you believe. As Paul wrote to the Corinthians, when you see Jesus for who he truly is, it will cause you to become like him from one degree of glory to the next. Whatever degree of glory you or I have grown into in our walk with God, there is more. There is always more opportunity to further renew our minds, to make them new again, to change what we believe about God and ourselves.

The next chapters each express something about who God is and how he is so much better than most of us know. It's going to take the lid off his goodness in your life and create opportunities for you to behold him as he truly is. His goodness will shape the way you think in your daily life in a way that will bring you freedom, confidence, and joy.

So get ready, because your journey toward becoming you is just beginning.

Chapter 2

THE TRUTH ABOUT GLORY

Generations of Christians have declared that we exist for God's glory. This is true, but what if one small shift in perspective could change what this means and how we think about who God is toward us? In reality, God's nature demands him to be focused on us. Far from making us prideful, this revelation is actually the key we need to help us follow God's plan to make us like him.

Civil war set the backdrop to the formation of one of the Western world's most influential documents on church belief, teachings, and practice. It took many meetings over the course of five years to craft this document before it was finally agreed upon and ratified even into law by two different national parliaments.³

I'm talking about the Westminster Confession of Faith, which was written almost four hundred years ago, during the English Civil War, almost as a treaty to secure Scotland's help against the king of England. It helped unite both nation's churches in what they confessed to believe and how they practiced their faith.

All this makes the Westminster Confession sound very important, doesn't it? It should, because it is important. Impressively, many denominations still hold to it today. That's some real lasting power, a testament usually reserved for documents that are really founded on the truth of Scripture. If it wasn't accurate to Scripture, it is simply too easy to read the Bible for yourself to see that it isn't and leave it behind.

I went to a college where the Westminster Confession was pretty important. While I never studied the document itself, I clearly remember the one phrase from it that I heard quoted most often (and it was quite often): "The chief end of man is to glorify God and enjoy him always." Every time you hear a professional athlete, high-profile celebrity, or even just the girl who sang a nice offertory on a Sunday morning deflect praise by saying, "I just have to give God all the glory," you are hearing someone who was influenced in some way by the sentiments expressed in this confession. In fact, chances are good that your beliefs have been influenced by this phrase whether you know it or not.

Now, before I go any further, I want to be clear here and say that I agree with every word in this statement. We should ascribe glory to God. What I don't agree with is what many people mean by it or how we have applied it.

DON'T REDEFINE GOD'S INTENT

Most Christians have an attitude toward God that centers around the revelation of God as both God and Lord—and he very clearly is both. But it's an attitude that has either forgotten or never discovered what God said about humankind right before he made us—that he made us to be like him. What happens, then, is that most Christians apply the truths of God's lordship in a way that actually prevents us from becoming like him. We might even think it irreverent to suggest we are created to become like him, as though our promotion to his likeness could somehow diminish his greatness.

We have this concept of humankind as so completely depraved and unregenerate that it keeps us from believing that God's work in our lives is to unite us with himself and make us like him. We isolate ourselves from God because of what we believe about ourselves.

All this comes together in a mindset toward God where, when we say we are created to glorify him, what we mean is that we are wicked, lowly, wretched sinners, and the only way we can glorify him is by dying to ourselves every day (even though it won't work and we'll sin anyway), and we'll work really hard to serve God (even though it's against our nature and we can't do it very well), and we feel like he just puts up with us (because, seriously, he's so holy and we're so sinful). So we try to glorify him by staying out of his way. We try to glorify him by talking about how weak and sinful we are.

It's hard to understand how it glorifies God, though, when we debase his chief creation, the ones he created to be in his image. Really, how does it glorify God when we reimagine ourselves to be more in Satan's image than God's?

Ultimately, we try to glorify God by placing him at the center of the universe so that everything revolves around him. Everything is about him. Everything good is for him. He deserves everything. He is worthy of it all!

And that right there is what's so tricky about how we Christians have sold out to a lie—it's because this is all in response to things that are actually true about God. He is worthy of it all! He does deserve every good thing! But his worthiness is not an excuse to redefine the purpose for our existence. It is not cause for a universal identity crisis among humankind. Instead, it's an invitation to explore, experience, and understand what causes him to be worthy of every good thing.

GOD ISN'T LIKE SATAN

We have a distinct problem when we say God's intent in creating us was to glorify himself. That's what most Christians I've known mean when they say, "The chief end of man is to glorify God and enjoy him always." They take this phrase and apply the first part to mean God's intent in creating us was to make worshipers. He was so worthy of worship that it was downright wrong for him to not be worshiped; therefore, he created humankind so he could have an army of worshipers. The devil came along and has been trying to steal for himself as many of God's worshipers as he can, attempting to take God's place. The second phrase seems to get lost entirely by this view, or it's simply pushed into life in heaven, leaving the sole focus of human life on this act of subjugating ourselves to the supreme, enthroned deity who is so worthy of worship that this purpose defines our entire existence.

But how can we really believe that when God himself said he made us to be like him? How can we believe God created us for the purpose of establishing a hierarchy that separates him from us when he embraced the identity "God with us" and sent his Spirit to make us his home, and when that same Spirit is continually working in us to conform us again to his image?

Hold on, though, because that's not even the biggest problem with saying God's intent in creating us was to glorify himself. The biggest problem here is that this intent would actually portray God as having the same character as Satan. Yes, I did just say what you think I said, but stick with me.

Ezekiel 28:11–19 gives us a clear description of Lucifer. Actually, it's a poem to mourn him because of the beauty he had but lost through corruption. This passage reveals Satan's motivation that drove him to fall: "Your heart was proud because of your beauty; you corrupted your wisdom for the sake of your splendor. I cast you to the ground; I exposed you before kings, to feast their eyes on you" (v. 17).

Satan's heart was proud because of his beauty, so he thought he deserved worship. He thought he was so beautiful that he should be exalted as the highest being in the universe, even higher than God. He corrupted his wisdom for the sake of his splendor, bending and perverting the know-how God endowed on him to focus it on glorifying and further beautifying himself.

This is the very attitude that caused Satan to fall. It is the belief and thought process that led to God himself casting Lucifer to the ground. Yet it is the exact same belief and thought process that many attribute to God as his motivation for creating humankind, excusing this unspeakable comparison by simply saying, "Well, God's worthy of that because it's true of him. Satan's not worthy. That's why it was wrong for him."

I'm sorry, but that's not good enough for me. I see a clear contrast between this description of Satan's heart—which was completely focused on his own glory, leading to God taking everything from him—and Paul's description of Jesus' heart:

> Have this mind among yourselves, which is yours in Christ Jesus, who, though he was in the form of God, did not count equality with God a thing to be grasped, but made himself nothing, taking the form of a servant, being born in the likeness of men. And being found in human form, he humbled himself by becoming obedient to the point of death, even death on a cross. Therefore God has highly exalted him and bestowed on him the name that is above every name, so that at the name of Jesus every knee should bow, in heaven and on earth and under the earth, and every tongue confess that Jesus Christ is Lord, to the glory of God the Father.—Philippians 2:5–11

These verses perfectly mirror the passage about Satan but also contrast with it at every point. Satan became proud because of his beauty, but Jesus considered equality with God as nothing to be held onto. Satan looked to exalt himself above God, but Jesus emptied himself of everything that made him equal to God. Satan perverted his wisdom to increase his splendor, but Jesus clothed himself with humanity and humbled himself to the point of crucifixion.

As their characters are different, so are the results God gives them. God threw Lucifer to earth, stripping him of his beauty and debasing him below all other created things, but he exalted Jesus above every other being so that every created thing would worship and bow before him. Note that it's God who does the debasing and exalting of these two characters, and it's not like he's playing favorites, as though the reason he debased Satan was because he perceived him as his rival or the reason he exalted Jesus was because he's his Son. No, the reason he debased Satan was his character, and the reason he exalted Jesus was his character.

Our conclusion is what should already be quite obvious: God is very much not like Satan. The two are polar opposites both in character and in the result that character brings. The trick for us as Christians is that too often we only focus on the result of Jesus' character and not his character itself. We emphasize his lordship without remembering the humility that placed him on the throne.

GOD'S DEFINITION OF GLORY

At the root of this is a misunderstanding of God's glory. It's true that most of the time when we use a word, we understand it by its primary meaning. If we do this for the word *glory*, we understand it to be something like a bright shining light, an overwhelming intensity of presence, or even a greatness of wealth and majesty. All of these are good definitions for glory, and all of the them are true of God. We can find numerous examples throughout Scripture to show this. However, when it comes to his own glory, God gives us a different definition.

The stage is Mount Sinai, a craggy shard of rock jutting up from the desert wasteland. The nation of Israel is gathered around the base of the mountain, having camped there for almost three months (it's been that long since the day God appeared on the mountain). A noise awakened the people that morning, a sound they had never heard before. It was a trumpet blast, but it never stopped. Instead, it only grew louder and louder. When they exited their tents to see where the trumpet sound came from, they saw the mountain aflame like an enormous kiln reaching up into heaven so high that the winds in the upper atmosphere captured the smoke and spread it across the sky. The earth beneath their feet shook, and when God spoke to them, it was with a voice like thunder.

Moses dared enter into the very heart of that furnace, not returning for forty days. When he did return, the people had forsaken the God on the mountain for an idol made of gold. Moses punished the people, then returned to the mountain. He spent a total of eighty days with God—eighty days surrounded by the perpetual nuclear blast of God's presence. God revealed to him heavenly blueprints for his earthly tabernacle filled with legendary artifacts like the ark of the covenant. And throughout those eighty days, Moses ate and drank nothing; God himself sustained him.

This is where God revealed his glory for what it truly is. This is where Moses, after having lived in this environment for nearly three months, made a bold request. He said to God, "Please show me your glory" (Exodus 33:18).

What astounds me the most about his request is that Moses somehow understood that the raw power saturating him upon Mount Sinai for eighty days was *not* God's glory. It seems to me that everything he saw during that time perfectly fits the description of everything we normally associate with God's glory, yet when Moses beheld it like none of us ever have, he knew there was something more.

God's response to Moses reveals the truth about his glory:

Moses said, "Please show me your glory." And he said, "I will make all my goodness pass before you and will proclaim before you my name 'The Lord.' And I will be gracious to whom I will be gracious, and will show mercy to whom I show mercy." —Exodus 33:18–19

When Moses asks to see God's glory, knowing all he had yet seen wasn't it, God told him he would cause all his goodness to pass before him. Let's sit on that for a second.

If you think about God, you'll realize that whatever word you use to describe him, he truly is the definition of that word. Holy. Righteous. Love. Mercy. It's not that these words describe him so much as that he is the embodiment of these words. The same is true of his goodness. God doesn't just *have* goodness; he *is* goodness!

As if this weren't enough, God emphasizes the entirety of his goodness he was about to show Moses. He said, "I will make *all* my goodness pass before you." This means that he is able to reveal only part of his goodness to us, and I think all of us could certainly say that's true. If I asked you what in your life reminds you of God's goodness, you would tell me something about it that I have never seen before. If we had a room full of people giving the same testimony, we would have a rich treasure full of his goodness revealed separately and partially to each one of us. But to Moses God said he would reveal all his goodness. That's absolutely incredible!

God continued beyond his promise to make all his goodness pass before Moses, saying that when he did so, he would proclaim his name, "The Lord." Now, this is how the translators write God's name down for us, putting it in all caps so we understand God isn't really saying the words, *The Lord*, but is instead actually saying, *I Am*.

When we rewrite the passage this way to say what God really said, we read, "I will make all my goodness pass before you and will proclaim my name, 'I Am.'" In other words, God was emphatically, as clearly as he possibly could, declaring to Moses that his glory is the reality that "He Is Good."

JESUS' REVELATION OF GLORY

When we understand God's definition of glory, the gospel makes so much more sense. One of the common ways for people to share the gospel begins with Romans 3:23, "For all have sinned and fall short of the glory of God." When someone uses this to present the gospel, it's usually to convince someone they are a sinner, but let's look at it with a fresh perspective now that we know what God's glory is.

We sin when we fall short of God's glory. In other words, anything that causes us to experience or express something short of God's goodness is sin. Jesus' life shows us how true this definition is. Start with John 1:14: "And the Word became flesh and dwelt among us, *and we have seen his glory, glory as of the only Son from the Father*, full of grace and truth." This is one of the statements from the Gospels that sums up the life of Jesus. The words John chose to describe Jesus' life tell us that Jesus' life perfectly displayed the glory of God.

Interestingly, Peter walked with Jesus through the same things for the same amount of time but chose different words when he summed up Jesus' life. When he addressed a house full of Gentiles for the first time, he described Jesus' life by saying, "God anointed Jesus of Nazareth with the Holy Spirit and with power. He went about *doing good* and healing all who were oppressed by the devil, for God was with him" (Acts 10:38).

These are two perspectives from two of the people who were most intimate with Jesus during his ministry on earth. They used different words to express what Jesus did. John was more mystical, as was his style, and Peter was more practical, as was his style, but they both said the same thing. John said Jesus revealed God's glory, and Peter said Jesus went about doing good. The good things Jesus did were how he revealed God's glory.

WHY GOD SENT HIS SON

Let me recap briefly. Yes, we are created to glorify God, but, no, that doesn't look like how we have traditionally lived it. Instead, we understand God's glory is the reality that he is goodness itself, declared by the Father and revealed in Jesus' life by all the good works he did everywhere he went.

But perhaps the most mind-blowing demonstration of God's glory is hidden in a passage already quoted, Philippians 2:5–11. This passage unlocked possibly the greatest and most personal mystery I ever asked God to help me understand.

The foundation for my dilemma started the summer after ninth grade. It was a time in my life when God clearly marked me with the revelation of knowing him as my intimate Daddy and me as his chosen son. God's work in my heart was so deep during this time that this is still the primary way I think of God today. The problem I had was that I knew God the Father had sent his Son, Jesus, to die. Complicating this was that I knew Jesus didn't always have a physical body—that there was a moment in time when he became incarnate.

I recognized that while God is one, somehow there was the mystery of how he exists in three persons, and that if the Son could become incarnate, why couldn't the Father? And if the Father could become incarnate and die for humankind, sparing his Son that torture, why didn't he? I questioned how much I could trust my Father if he was willing to send his children to die, especially if it were true that he could have just as easily died for them or saved them from death but chose to send them anyway.

I knew this characterization of God didn't match who I knew him to be, but I still didn't understand the mystery. It left me walking wholeheartedly, yet still a little tenderly, in my relationship with Father God.

Now, let's look at the passage that I said helped me out of all this:

> Have this mind among yourselves, which is yours in Christ Jesus, who, though he was in the form of God, did not count equality with God a thing to be grasped, but made himself nothing, taking the form of a servant, being born in the likeness of men. And being found in human form, he humbled himself by becoming obedient to the point of death, even death on a cross. Therefore God has highly exalted him and bestowed on him the name that is above every name, so that at the name of Jesus every knee should bow, in heaven and on earth and under the earth, and every tongue confess that Jesus Christ is Lord, to the glory of God the Father.—Philippians 2:5–11

Earlier, I talked about how this passage contrasts perfectly with another passage to show that Jesus and Satan have opposite characters leading to opposite results. Satan promoted himself and was cast out of heaven as a profane thing. Jesus humbled himself to serve others and was exalted above every creature throughout time in the entire universe. The only constants are that God set the values for how to be promoted in heaven and that he is the one doing the promoting.

You might not realize it, but you actually just read the answer to my dilemma. God knew the value system that gets someone promoted in heaven. Jesus said it himself—the least become the greatest and the greatest become the least (Matthew 19:30 and 20:25–28). God the Father knew that if he was the one to become human and die on a cross for humankind, saving his Son from doing it, it would result in him sitting on the highest throne with the greatest name, and however this works within the mystery of the Trinity, Jesus would be sitting on the outside, forever lower than his Father.

But that didn't fit the heart of heaven either. The Father wouldn't want the Son to remain lower, and this passage clearly tells us so. Look at the very end, at the part when every eye is on Jesus, every mouth is worshiping him, and every physical and spiritual form is prostrate before him. When that happens, when all attention—and I mean *all* attention—is on the Son, that is to the glory of God the Father.

Did you notice that the Father wasn't even mentioned by name until the very end of the passage? This passage, from beginning to almost end, is completely about Jesus! But when everyone worships the Son and no one is even thinking of the Father, when the Father has so exalted the Son that he is now on the outside watching fondly, that is when the Father is most glorified. That is God's system of glory! That is what God means when he says he will be glorified!

And, bringing us back to where we started, that has to be what we mean when we say we live to glorify God. We cannot glorify God by demeaning ourselves and our fellow men and women around the world. We cannot glorify God by focusing on sinfulness or failures or any of that sort of thing. The only way for us to glorify God is to allow him to exalt us. Yes, we glorify God by allowing him to exalt us, to show us his goodness, to bless us and serve us and make us his children!

Yes, just as I quoted in Philippians, we are to have the same attitude as Christ Jesus, but there is a distinct process to how God intends it to happen. Keep reading, because we'll get there, though, again, not fully in this chapter.

HUMILITY KNOWS HOW TO RECEIVE

Christianity has done a great job training people to be servants. We know very well the values of serving, and we do a great job of offering people places to serve within our local church bodies. Within that culture of service—which is a good and biblical culture to have—we have not done a good job teaching all the servants how to receive.

The apostle Peter struggled with this even in the moment when Jesus was teaching him the value of service. Peter may have argued with the other disciples about who was the greatest among one another, but he had the pecking order figured out enough to know Jesus was at the top. So while he didn't volunteer to wash anyone else's feet, he didn't feel right letting Jesus wash his.

Many Christians have the same problem in the way they relate to God. They're so oriented toward serving God that they become uncomfortable with the idea of God serving them. Sure, they're fine with Jesus serving them by dying for them. That's in the past. It's done and accomplished, so now Jesus can just be Lord and that's it. We serve, he rules. It's a very comfortable, clearly defined relationship that way, and it makes us feel secure in our role.

The problem is that God never changed. Leadership within God's kingdom still expresses itself through service. Just as we can never be promoted to a place where it's okay for us to stop serving, neither can Jesus be promoted to a throne so high that he will stop serving those below him. It's not like he died to establish a pension in heaven so he could retire when he ascended from earth.

We need to understand this, because while *we* might serve one another out of a sense of duty or knowing it's the right thing to do, *Jesus serves because it's his nature to do so.* Jesus didn't act out of character when he humbled himself to take on human form. He wasn't pretending to be a servant when he washed his disciples' feet.

Rather, he was showing us what God is always like more clearly than we had ever seen before. Jesus even told us so, saying, "Whoever has seen me has seen the Father" (John 14:9). The apostle John wrote it again, saying, "No one has ever seen God; the only God, who is at the Father's side, he has made him known" (John 1:18) and making this single point a major theme throughout his gospel. Even more, Paul wrote, "He is the image of the invisible God" (Colossians 1:15).

Jesus showed us what God is like, and God doesn't change. He didn't temporarily become a servant for thirty-three years, teaching us to serve and love one another, and telling us that servants are the greatest in his kingdom, only to return to his primary character traits of authoritarian rule and lording his power over people once he physically left our planet.

This means we need to expect that God will still serve us today! And it means we need to learn how to receive this from him. Of course we don't stop serving him in return, but we can't live like service is a one-way street in our relationship with God. Yes, we serve him, and yes, he serves us. It goes both ways, and it has to.

THE WHOLE FARM IS YOURS

Our Father serves us. We have to see this in his nature, knowing that this truth about him will never change. It is true about him forever. There is no point in eternity in heaven when God will stop being Lord, and there is no point when he will stop being a servant. They are both true and will coexist eternally, just as they always have. God will not change.

I say we have to see this in him because our ability to become who we were born to be depends on it. Our witness to the world depends on it. Our ability to walk out the reality that we are children of God and created to be like him depends on it.

Jesus' parable of the prodigal son helps us understand what's at stake. The whole story is found in Luke 15, but I'll summarize it. One day when he was teaching, Jesus told the story of a man who had two sons. The younger son approached him and asked to receive his portion of the inheritance. Despite the fact that this basically meant his son was telling him he wished he were dead, the father granted the request. He gave his son his inheritance, and the son left to seek and spend his fortune somewhere else.

It wasn't long before the young man had wasted all he had on prostitutes and parties. When his money dried up, so did his shallow friendships, and he found himself very alone. At his deepest moment of desperation, he determined to return home to become his father's servant so he would at least have food. When he arrived home, however, the father embraced him and fully restored him, throwing him a party to celebrate his return.

This all sets the stage for what happens with the older brother, which is what I'm going to focus on. The older brother returns home from a long day in the fields and inquires what all the to-do is about. When he finds it's for his no-good brother, he refuses to join the party. Jesus says this about the father's response:

> "His father came out and entreated him, but he answered his father, 'Look, these many years I have served you, and I never disobeyed your command, yet you never gave me a young goat, that I might celebrate with my friends. But when this son of yours came, who has devoured your property with prostitutes, you killed the fattened calf for him!' And he said to him, 'Son, you are always with me, and all that is mine is yours. It was fitting to celebrate and be glad, for this your brother was dead, and is alive; he was lost, and is found.'"—Luke 15:28–32

If you've been around church long enough, you've heard this story before. The application that was probably made from the story was evangelistic in nature: don't be like the older brother and pout when God's prodigal children come to him; instead rejoice and reach out to those who need him. As I keep saying about so many things, this is good and true, but it isn't all there is to see here.

This application does a great job at seeing the father's words, "It was fitting to celebrate and be glad," but we need to also see his profound words that come right before that: "Son, you are always with me, and all that is mine is yours."

One of the most deeply transformational moments of my life happened one night shortly after I was married. I lay in bed, staring at the ceiling, when suddenly I saw in the Spirit something flying down through the ceiling and into my heart. Before I knew what happened, I heard the Lord speak to me some of the clearest words I have ever heard him say. He said, "The whole farm is yours!" It was so clear that it was as if he were shouting.

Immediately, I had so much filling my mind to know what he meant as those words exploded in me, that I couldn't journal fast enough. I stopped writing and started typing, and then I typed four full pages—nearly enough words to equal a whole chapter of this book. I knew I had just experienced a powerful encounter with God's Spirit of adoption, marking me as his son in a way that had always been true of me, but I hadn't known it within myself to such a depth before. I knew that God's "farm" includes basically everything and that God was simply quoting his own Scripture to me to help me understand how big of a blank check he has offered his children.

This is the piece the older brother was truly missing. You see, while the younger son had no character to make use of his inheritance, at least he knew he was a son. The older brother had so embraced the role of a servant that he had forgotten what it meant to be a son.

Many Christians have done the same thing, so fully embracing the value of servanthood that they don't know how to be God's son or daughter. They know how to steward many things, but they don't know how to inherit anything. They don't understand how powerful it is to hear, "Son, you are always with me, and all that I have is yours." They are so focused on serving the Father that they don't know how to receive from him.

Because—and here's the kicker—the older brother already had access to everything. He was waiting for permission, but permission had already been given simply because he was a son. He perceived such a gap between him and his father. The father ruled the property; the son served. But the father eliminated the gap—"Son, you are always with me"—and he served his son as an equal—"and all that I have is yours."

This is so important! Unless the older brother in the story can understand the truths the father is telling him, he will never actually be ready to come into his inheritance. This is the paradox of the parable—as children of God, we need to have the character of the older brother but the identity of the younger. Only when we put both of them together will we understand our sonship to receive from our Father and have the character to use our inheritance to serve, just like Jesus does.

LET YOUR WALLS DOWN

In the end, this really doesn't have to be so difficult. God already possesses everything he has called us to, and he's the only one who does. How else can we possibly become children of God created to become like him except by receiving it from him?

What I think has kept us from receiving the fullness of these from our Father in the past is this strange mix of seeing ourselves as unworthy and perceiving him as either unwilling or disinterested. It's true that we might be unworthy, but that has never seemed to matter to God. The first child he ever took for himself began as a lump of dirt. You can't get much less worthy than that. We need to stop worrying about our worthiness and realize that, worthy or not, God chose us, loves us, and will serve us forever throughout eternity.

It is only when we embrace this truth that we will be able to become like him. The whole world groans in waiting for the sons of God to be revealed, and it won't happen until God's children realize his heart toward us. We have to let the weight of his heart settle upon us, because until we realize how significant we are to him, we won't let ourselves feel that significant about ourselves and we won't live out that significance to the world that needs it.

The world is waiting for us to believe in ourselves the way that God believes in us. They are waiting for us to let the significance of God's heart toward us transform us into who we were created to be. They are waiting for us to let our walls down and allow God to serve us.

Chapter 3

WHO SAYS?

> Many voices speak to us every day, trying to convince us to follow them. Most of those voices tell us how terrible we are, continually tearing us down to keep us from becoming who God made us to be. The key to our destiny, then, is to learn what God says about us and cling to his voice relentlessly. There is only one voice that matters—our Father's.

When God showed me the vision of his Bride that I described in the introduction to this book, it powerfully stirred something inside of me. I've come to realize that this intense rousing is surprisingly simple to articulate. All I have to do is say, "I believe in you."

It's true. I don't care who you are, where you've been, what you've done, or how cliché this sounds—I have never met a person I didn't believe in. I believe in absolutely everyone, and the reason I so fervently and passionately believe in everyone is because I have seen a glimpse of their potential.

I so believe in people that I almost always believe in them more than they believe in themselves. God gave me this passion. There's no question in my mind about it, and I can tell you why: it's because God believes in you. He is your maker, and he knows the dreams he has in his heart for you. He knows your potential and keenly understands the value of your life.

I know without a shadow of a doubt that you are made in God's image and that there is something in how he made you and in who he designed you to become that will reveal God in a way that no one else ever could. I know you're a treasure crafted by the hand of God himself. I know you uniquely bear his image and display him like no one else. There really is something supernaturally and indescribably wonderful and powerful in that.

This is how I look at every person I pass on the street. When I look around the food court at a mall, this is often what I think about. I wonder, *Who are these people? What are they created to become? Are they fulfilled in their life? Do they know who God made them to be? How can I help wake them up and set them free? How can I connect them to the one voice that can unlock everything their heart desires?*

My thoughts are so filled with the magnitude of God that I continually marvel that the people around me are the key to me understanding the fullness of who God is, that without them becoming who they are created to be, those mysteries about himself that God designed them to carry will remain hidden.

WHICH VOICE DO YOU BELIEVE?

That's why I so deeply believe in everyone. So why don't all these people believe in themselves? It's because they, like all of us, have to one degree or another believed a voice that has lied to them, and there are many voices that do.

I'm not talking only about spiritual voices here, like how Satan deceived Eve into believing she needed to make up for her lack. That voice led her and Adam into less than God created them to become, and similar voices certainly try to speak to each one of us today. Even Jesus heard demonic voices trying to speak doubt and deception into his soul.

But many times, the voice that speaks loudest and carries the most influence is the voice of history. We all have experience with our own failures, limitations, rejections, and insults. Every one of us has had times when we knew what to do but didn't or couldn't do it. All of us know what it's like to want something but have it taken away from us or given to another person. We all have felt the sting of scorn, derision, and mocking for any number of things and any number of reasons. Unfortunately, these experiences are nearly universal.

Because of these experiences, we all carry shame and condemnation. As I wrote before, research shows that every person experiences shame (except for psychopaths). Condemnation, shame, and the experience of failure can sometimes lead to hopelessness and fear. Having fallen down so many times, it can be hard to keep getting up, especially in the face of opposition.

Those other voices are quick to jump on us when we're down. We might have lived the majority of our lives as an optimistic, happy-go-lucky kind of person, but one season of difficulty can begin to eat away at our confidence. One day we have the simple thought, *Maybe I'm not as great as I thought I was,* and sometimes that can be all the invitation the demonic realm needs to come water those doubts and feed that shame. It can start a downward spiral that leads us away from who we were created to be, slowly creating a prison around our soul that echoes, "Who, me? There's no way I would ever do that! Do you know what happened to me the last time I tried to do that? Why would I be stupid enough to try something like that again?"

I know what these voices sound like. I've heard them so often that it feels like I hear them on more days than I don't hear them. Everyone knows what these voices sound like, if they'll admit it. Most people hear them so often that they just think they are their own thoughts. Everyone knows these voices, and everyone knows the difficult emotions that come with them.

What not everyone knows is that these voices sound nothing like God. After all, God spoke his opinion of us from the very beginning. He declared the thoughts of his heart about us, that he made us to be like him. He demonstrated in the most extreme fashion that he never changed his mind about us by suffering and dying on the cross for us. He established our value by his own independent estimation—the only one that counts—and determined that we are worth his life, that our lives are worth more than his.

His voice is the one that declares our value! When his voice so starkly contrasts with the voices we're used to hearing, we have to question the voices. When we realize that God believes in us, we have to wonder why we doubt ourselves.

GOD TRUMPS YOUR HISTORY

The apostle Paul's life is a great story to help us see someone successfully walk through the process of overcoming history to reach his destiny. Paul—then known by his Jewish name, Saul—was the premier teacher of the law in all Israel, tutored by the very best and most respected Pharisee of his day.

Saul hated Jesus, and, well, that's not a good way to start. He hated Jesus and everyone who followed him so much that Acts 9:1 says he breathed out threats and murder against the church. Think about that. His hatred for Christians was so strong that it was as if every breath he breathed was laced with murder toward them. That's a passionate hatred!

When the believers fled Jerusalem, hoping to escape Saul's wrath, Saul obtained permission to chase them down with warrants to bring them back to face his "justice." On such an errand, he traveled to Damascus, and on that road Jesus appeared to him. He simply said, "I am Jesus, whom you are persecuting. But rise and enter the city, and you will be told what you are to do" (Acts 9:5–6). Having been struck blind by the vision, Paul's companions guided him into the city and he waited.

Meanwhile, God appeared to man named Ananias, telling him where he could find Saul and instructing him to go heal his blindness. Ananias protested, "But, God, many have told me about him. He has a bad reputation. If I go there he might kill me!"

God responded, basically saying, "Don't worry about it. I have chosen him."

WHO SAYS?

This apparently was good enough for Ananias, because the story tells us he got up immediately, went to Saul, and healed him. But this whole story is amazing to me because of how people respond to God's voice.

First, Saul had staked his career, his reputation, and even his life on this belief: Jesus isn't God. Everything he did centered around him believing that to be the truth. Yet when God spoke, everything changed. He realized his old ways of thinking were wrong and that those Christians had been right the whole time. Second, everything Ananias said to God about Saul was true. He had a reputation among the Christians, and it obviously wasn't a good one, and deservedly so. Ananias didn't need to make up excuses or lies about Saul to try to find a way out of this assignment.

Yet when God spoke again, saying, "I have chosen him," Ananias suddenly didn't care about Saul's history anymore. He so believed God's words and trusted his ability to hear God clearly that he staked his life on it. Honestly, I laugh every time I think about his dramatic turn around.

God said, "Go heal Saul."

Ananias said, "But, Lord, I've heard about him, and he might kill me."

God said, "Yes, but I say I've chosen him."

Ananias said, "Oh, okay, that's good enough for me. I'll go risk my life then, because you told me to."

For all of us, this is a powerful lesson that God's opinion trumps both our history and our reputation. If God disagrees with our history, it's our history that's wrong.

Yes, I know that your history and mine are factual events, but God's words have creative power. If he says you aren't the person you used to be, then his words cause you to become transformed. God cannot lie. Even if he were to say something that wasn't true, his very act of saying it would cause it to become true as soon as he said it. So I repeat, if God disagrees with your history, it's your history that's wrong!

BECOME YOU

HANDLING FAILURE

Going back to Saul's story, it looks like things have turned around for him, doesn't it? If you keep reading through Acts 9, you'll see that as zealous as he was to persecute Jesus, he is now equally as zealous to proclaim Jesus. This looks like the beginning of his promising life as a missionary to the nations, right? Well, not exactly:

> But Saul increased all the more in strength, and confounded the Jews who lived in Damascus by proving that Jesus was the Christ. When many days had passed, the Jews plotted to kill him, but their plot became known to Saul. They were watching the gates day and night in order to kill him, but his disciples took him by night and let him down through an opening in the wall, lowering him in a basket.—Acts 9:22–25

Saul's great beginning to ministry quickly led to the first plot against his life by the Jews. Before he knew it, Saul found himself friendless. He couldn't stay with his disciples in Damascus or the Jews would kill him, so he returned to Jerusalem where the disciples were still afraid of him. And, really, think about it. Imagine that someone's every breath spouted murder at you, and after that person mercifully disappeared for a few months, they came back wanting to be your friend. It wasn't exactly easy for those early believers to trust Saul.

Thankfully, Barnabas took hold of him and brought him to the apostles, sharing his testimony with them about how Jesus had transformed his life. This again sounds like an encouraging breakthrough for a man who would become a renowned apostle and missionary, but the problem was—well, to be honest, Saul was the problem.

> [Saul] went in and out among them at Jerusalem, preaching boldly in the name of the Lord. And he spoke and disputed against the Hellenists. But they were seeking to kill him. And when the brothers learned this, they brought him down to Caesarea and

sent him off to Tarsus. So the church throughout all Judea and Galilee and Samaria had peace and was being built up. And walking in the fear of the Lord and in the comfort of the Holy Spirit, it multiplied.—Acts 9:28–31

It's easy to see the repeated pattern in Saul's life. He was so zealous against Jesus that he stirred up persecution against Christians. Then he became so zealous for Jesus that he still stirred up persecution against Christians, especially against himself, managing to incite two different murder plots against his life in two different cities in what was likely no more than one year's time. That has to set some sort of infamous record for stirring up trouble!

In the middle of all that trouble comes one small word: *so*. "So the church ... had peace" (9:31). In other words, once they finally got rid of Saul, the church as a whole finally had peace. He was the sole reason for their trouble! As soon as he was gone, the church had peace, was built up, and multiplied.

Can you imagine how you would feel if a church multiplied and became healthier simply because you left town? What would it be like to have done almost as much damage to the church when you were for it as when you were against it? How would you handle this kind of situation when some of the first words God said about you were, "He is a chosen instrument of mine to carry my name before the Gentiles and kings and the children of Israel" (Acts 9:15)? How could you manage such a wonderful promise in contrast with such massive failures?

Unfortunately, the Bible doesn't tell us the specifics of how Saul handled that terrible first year of his Christian life. It does tell us, however, that it was about fourteen more years before he left with Barnabas on his first missionary journey. It's pretty clear that Saul changed quite a bit over those years, during which time he began using his Roman name, Paul. Interestingly, Paul means "small," which could tell us that Paul learned a lot of humility in those years.

He learned how to restrain himself from simply being a bull in a china shop everywhere he went. He learned how to serve and how to follow, as evidenced by how he is first reintroduced to us. When Paul and Barnabas first set out to the nations, Scripture gives us their names in reverse, Barnabas then Paul, indicating that Barnabas was the leader and Paul was the supporter.

How many times during those fourteen years do you think Paul questioned God's plan for his life? How many times did he look back on that first year that had been so full of failure? How much did he have to wrestle with the fiery passion that defined who he was to make himself just stay put and follow God through the process?

Really try to feel what this would have been like. Imagine your life fourteen years ago to gain perspective on just how long that is and how much people change in that amount of time. Can you begin to understand something of the process Paul went through? He was very much not an overnight success.

STICK WITH THE PROCESS

Thankfully, and praise God for this, he did stick with the process, learned from his failures, and stayed the course to become the man God created him to be. We see clearly from his life that there is a process to our identity, and there's no way out of it. When God makes us new creations in Christ, we are infants. We have some growing, learning, and maturing to do.

Along the way we will sometimes fail at things we felt we were supposed to do. It's not a fun realization, but it's the truth. If you haven't failed at what you felt you were supposed to do, then you probably haven't tried either hard or often enough yet. I know this is true because none of us were born experts at who God created us to become. Oftentimes the only school available to us is experience, and that means trying things we've never tried before, which means we're not going to be very good at it all the time, which means we will sometimes fail. But that failure is also the only way we'll learn to grow and become strong in our identity. Hear that again: failure is the only way you will become you.

As I said, failure isn't fun. I personally don't like even the idea of it. I'm still getting over my fear of failure, to be honest. But at least I know enough about how important it is to embrace it when it happens. I also know there are three common but wrong assumptions about failure.

First, there are some people who act as though it's impossible to fail—almost as if they don't recognize when they are failing. For one reason or another, they live in denial about their failures. Whether they're genuinely deceived to the point of ignorance or whether they're just so afraid of failure that they won't acknowledge it when it happens, they refuse to see failure in their lives. As a consequence, they live as though their decisions don't matter.

The problem here is that if you act like consequences don't matter, you will never be able to accomplish anything of consequence. Your life cannot amount to much. You may be able to avoid the weight or burden that comes with responsibility, but you'll also simultaneously avoid the impact that responsibility can bring, from the simplest level of raising a healthy family to the more complicated opportunities around you. You have to be willing to acknowledge failure and learn from it, or you simply won't become all you were born to be.

Second, some people are so afraid of failure that it paralyzes them from making decisions. They are so terrified that they might pick the wrong direction at a fork in the road of life that they stay at the intersection forever, refusing to move forward. Obviously, this group of people will also ironically fail to become who they were created to be, because they never complete the journey of getting there. God is so very merciful to hold our hands tenderly as we grow toward our identity, but there are still moments that demand boldness and courage.

One of the most often repeated commands in Scripture is, "Fear not, don't be afraid!" God has always known that the path he calls us to walk requires courage. If we let him, he will always give us the strength we need for each day, no matter the difficulty or challenge, and teach us to think as he does, to see our battles as he does, so that we can overcome one after the other with his power.

Third, some people are so ashamed of their failures that they think they've already blown it. When I was taking theology classes in Bible college, my professor told our class that one of the most common letters they receive is from people who are concerned they have committed the unpardonable sin Jesus mentions in Mark 3:28–29. It was so common that this professor said he kept a form letter on hand to send in reply (by the way, his answer was that if you're concerned about whether you've committed that sin, then you haven't).

Listen, the list of major screw-ups God has used is extensive. Noah drank too much. Abraham lied. Moses, David, and Paul were all murderers, and David was an adulterer as well. Elijah and Timothy were afraid. Peter denied Jesus three times. Paul left the church better off when he got out of town. Rahab was a prostitute. Jeremiah was an uneducated kid. Gideon hid from his enemies. The list goes on and on. Choose your favorite Bible hero and you'll find a fault somewhere in their character. Almost all of them failed in some way at some point in their story, and many failed repeatedly. But God still used them.

My point is this: Choices do matter, but failure isn't fatal. Paul could have said, "But God, I just keep making messes everywhere I go. You really don't want to send me anywhere else!" Instead, he let God restore him from his postsalvation failures and went on to become the man who planted churches throughout Asia Minor and wrote so much of our New Testament. I'll tell you what, no one saw that legacy coming in Paul's future when he was terrorizing the church *as a Christian*!

If Paul had let failure stop him, that legacy never would have happened. Don't let failure stop your legacy. Allow God to restore you, because your future is always brighter than your past.

Chapter 4

SONS, NOT SINNERS

One thing keeps Christians trapped in failure more than anything else, and it's all one big lie. This lie convinces God's children they are still enslaved to sin to such an extent that they embrace it as their identity, calling themselves sinners. The truth of God's Word, however, gives us a new name and a new identity as new creations. This new life returns us to God's intent—that we would be made in his image.

It's been said that if you tie up an elephant when it is a baby and still relatively weak, attaching it to a stake in the ground with a rope around its leg, then when it is full grown it will still let itself be tied to that simple stake.

Obviously, a mature elephant could break the rope or rip the stake right out of the ground. What could restrain an infant elephant could by no means hold back an adult, at least not physically. The trick is that the restraint is entirely in the elephant's mind. It thinks it's stuck in the present because that rope kept it stuck in the past. Its past failures at gaining freedom have it convinced that it would still be a failure today.

This trick works on humans too. It's not an exaggeration to say that every Christian is held back from their full potential simply because of lies they believe about themselves. Some mindset has convinced them they are a failure or has robbed them of hope in some certain area of their life. Or some experience in their past has caused something to always be associated with pain for them. Either way, that person is like a chained elephant.

IT'S A TRAP

In church culture, there is one pervasive mindset that prevents people from moving past their failures more than any other. Honestly, that might not even put it in strong-enough language, because this mindset doesn't just keep people tied to their history; it also teaches them to make it their identity.

I remember an assignment in my high school philosophy class where the teacher handed out a one-page story that described a community of people who were happy, content, friendly, and safe. They lived life at a slow pace and made time for the people around them. This all changed when someone invented something called a RAC. This new device enabled people to travel faster and farther, and accomplish more things with a broader group of people. It didn't take long before everyone used a RAC. But it didn't come without a cost. These devices created much more pollution than what the people had used before, and they were less safe because of the speed at which they moved. Some people even died because of them, yet they all persisted in using them.

My teacher asked the class what we thought about these people. Almost every student talked about how stupid they were, seeming to trade every good thing for every bad thing with little benefit in return. He let these students dig themselves a big hole before asking one particular student what he thought.

That student said, "Everything my classmates have said makes sense, and in the story it does sound like those people are crazy. But as you read it, you realize that when they talk about a RAC, it's just 'car' spelled backward, and everything they say about a RAC is true about a car. Then you realize the people in the story aren't made up. They're us."

I feel like I could write a similar story about the mindset I'm about to explain to you, a story that shows how much this mindset robs from everyone who has it. Consider that this mindset, as I said, traps people in their history of failures. That means it binds them forever to shame and condemnation. It forces them to identify with the lowest moments of their lives and consider the best and highest moments as mere aberrations.

This mindset teaches those who have it to declare over themselves a name God never gave them, an alias that subjugates them to a lesser life. It leads them by faith into more failure, because it gives no hope or expectation for anything better.

A mindset this bad, you would think, would be easy to see for what it is so that believers would root it out and renounce it from their lives. Quite to the contrary, however, entire denominations throughout the world claim this mindset as one of their core doctrines.

WHAT "ALL" COVERS

The mindset I'm talking about is the belief that we are still sinners. It's perpetuated by men and women who say, "I'm just a sinner saved by grace," and it focuses solely on our experience of being imperfect, rather than on the biblical truth of how transformed we already are.

We begin discipling people into this mindset early, starting even before they are saved, in the way we present the gospel to them. If you have been trained in how to present the gospel to someone, chances are pretty good you were taught to use Romans 3:23: "For all have sinned and fall short of the glory of God."

As with any passage, the context for this verse matters. Here's the entire passage:

> But now the righteousness of God has been manifested apart from the law, although the Law and the Prophets bear witness to it—the righteousness of God through faith in Jesus Christ for all who believe. For there is no distinction: for *all* have sinned and fall short of the glory of God, and are justified by his grace

as a gift, through the redemption that is in Christ Jesus, whom God put forward as a propitiation by his blood, to be received by faith.—Romans 3:21–25

The main thought of this entire passage isn't about sin at all, but instead about the righteousness we gain by faith in Christ Jesus. To help drive this home, notice one small but important detail. Do you see how there is no period after the word *all* that I italicized, not until the very end of the passage? What that means is this little word *all* applies to everything that comes after it. Should we see what makes the list?

First, all have sinned. Yes, this is what it says, and yes, it is important for us to know. No one is exempt from sin—except Jesus. Just as we present in the gospel of salvation, this means we all need Jesus. In fact, we need Jesus in order to make the core truths of this passage apply to us, as we'll see. However, the fact that all have sinned remains only a small part of what we learn from Paul in these verses.

Second, all are justified. This is a judicial term that means someone had a sentence justly due against them because of a crime committed, but their debt is forgiven and wiped away; they are justified. This word tells us that our sins are forgiven. This is a precious word! And this is a word that, according to this verse, belongs to all. More than that, "all are" does not say "all will be." It means the same thing as "everyone now." God's justification and forgiveness hangs over every person, waiting only for them to receive it. It then immediately becomes a now, present-day truth in their life.

Third, all have been redeemed. This word tells us we used to be slaves to sin, but Jesus' death purchased our freedom. Now we belong to no one but him, and there is no control over us except his righteousness. This is a word we need to understand more deeply, because this very mindset I'm talking about still believes we are slaves to sin, as though we have not yet been redeemed, pushing off the power of Christ's redemption until we physically die to go to heaven. We'll get more into this in just a bit.

Fourth, all are qualified to receive the benefit of the propitiation found in Jesus' blood. *Propitiation* is a word that took me a long time to figure out, but it's actually pretty simple. In basic terms, it means that a deity was justifiably wrathful but now his wrath is appeased. Propitiation does that, it appeases God's wrath. This means God isn't angry with you, or anyone else has believed in Jesus. Let that sink into your soul: God has never once ever been angry with you since you first turned to him, and anytime you thought he was angry with you, it was all a lie to steal life from you. That is some really good news!

Finally, all this is to be received by faith. This means that all these things, these three incredible promises—God's justification, redemption, and propitiation—are all present realities hanging over every person's life, but not every person has grabbed ahold of them to benefit from them yet.

I like to compare this to electricity in my walls. I can't see the electricity, and because I can't see it, I could doubt you if you tried to convince me that my house was already wired for me to use it. But if I believe you, I step out in trust to plug into an outlet. Suddenly the power within my home surges forward to bring me light, heat and cold, and, best of all, to make my coffee pot work.

Eventually, people run out of time to put their faith in what Jesus has already done for us, and their choice or lack thereof does have eternal consequence. This is the reason why we have to evangelize and help the lost become found.

However, my concern is that we have a whole lot of Christians who still don't believe all this passage tells us. They only believe "all have sinned," and as far as they are concerned, they are still sinners. They know they are saved, yes—but they only see themselves as saved from the death sin brings and not from the power of sin itself. This leaves them trapped in sin, stuck with their failure, and bound to shame and condemnation.

SINNERS NO MORE

Most Christians, if they think about theology at all, would say they know Jesus' forgiveness sets them free from shame and condemnation. But what I know from having lived with Christians for more than thirty years is that nearly every Christian I have ever known is filled with shame, regardless of what they say they believe. They are keenly aware of their failures. In fact, it is this very awareness that causes them to have a belief that says, "I'm still a sinner."

It is certainly true that all have sinned, but thanks to Jesus, it is no longer true that all are sinners. This is an emphatic biblical teaching, as I'm about to show you, starting with what I already taught from Romans 3 and continuing with Romans 6.

This incredible chapter begins with some of the best news we can ever hear: we are already dead. Listen for yourself:

> What shall we say then? Are we to continue in sin that grace may abound? By no means! How can we who died to sin still live in it? Do you not know that all of us who have been baptized into Christ Jesus were baptized into his death? We were buried therefore with him by baptism into death, in order that, just as Christ was raised from the dead by the glory of the Father, we too might walk in newness of life.—Romans 6:1–4

Do you realize what you just read? Paul just told us that it is impossible for us to continue sinning. How else do you understand his rhetorical question, "How can we who died to sin still live in it?" The answer is obvious. We can't still live in sin. Why? Because we already died to it.

Once you die, you have no further access to the world in which you used to live. If a person dies, you can't have a conversation with them anymore. You can't go to the mall with them, or to the movies, or to play golf. You can't have any further relationship with them. They are dead. Paul tells us that this perfectly describes our relationship to sin.

So, how can this be true? Paul answers this for us as well by asking another question: "Do you not know that all of us who have been baptized into Christ Jesus were baptized into his death?" This means that if you have been baptized, you were united with Jesus' death. His death became your death, not as a promise for the future but as an experience that happened on your behalf two thousand years ago and became a present-day reality the moment you were baptized.

I understand this might seem confusing. You don't remember dying, and neither do I, but nevertheless we both did, assuming that we have both been baptized. This is the truth, whether it makes sense or not. It's like when I began learning algebra and couldn't understand for the life of me how x and y could possibly be a number and not a letter. I never did understand how x and y are sometimes numbers, but eventually I accepted that they sometimes are whether I understood how that transformation happened or not.

If you were to continue reading Romans 6, you would find there are at least thirty-four references to having died with Jesus, having been raised with Jesus, being free from the power of sin, being commanded to stop sinning, or being slaves to God's righteousness. Thirty-four! All of these emphatically tell us that we are truly free from sin.

WHAT ABOUT OUR "OLD MAN"?

So why do so many people teach that we are still sinners? Is there somewhere in the Bible they get this from? Well, yes, there is one main place I know of that could be interpreted to say that we are still sinners and still have an "old nature" or the "flesh" that drags us into habits we despise. This passage is a little long, but it's worth reading all the way through:

> For we know that the law is spiritual, but I am of the flesh, sold under sin. I do not understand my own actions. For I do not do what I want, but I do the very thing I hate. Now if I do what I do not want, I agree with the law, that it is good. So now it is no longer I who do it, but sin that dwells within me. For I know that nothing good dwells in me, that is, in my flesh. For I have the desire to do what is right, but not the ability to carry it out. For I do not do the good I want, but the evil I do not want is what I keep on doing. Now if I do what I do not want, it is no longer I who do

it, but sin that dwells within me. So I find it to be a law that when I want to do right, evil lies close at hand. For I delight in the law of God, in my inner being, but I see in my members another law waging war against the law of my mind and making me captive to the law of sin that dwells in my members. Wretched man that I am! Who will deliver me from this body of death? Thanks be to God through Jesus Christ our Lord! So then, I myself serve the law of God with my mind, but with my flesh I serve the law of sin.—Romans 7:14–25

I still remember clearly where I was when I read this passage for the first time and it clicked with me. I was in my college prayer chapel, sitting on the first stair where a small platform rose up against the back wall. Most likely, Passion's first worship compilation album was playing on the CD player as the world was first discovering who Chris Tomlin, Matt Redman, and David Crowder were.

When I read this passage, it was as if heaven opened above me and the light of God came down to comfort my anguished and tortured soul. Finally, I had words to express the struggle I had fought for years! Even better, I had good company. I mean, if the apostle Paul struggled with sin to such a degree, then at least it must be normal for Christians to experience this, right?

Most likely, this is how so many Christians have latched on to this passage and why they hold it so dearly. The ministry of commiseration gives them comfort to keep pressing on in their daily struggle with sin. It helps them forgive themselves when they fail instead of wholeheartedly caving in to the shame and condemnation they feel. That certainly was the case for me.

Thankfully, someone explained the context of this passage to me more fully so that I saw not only that I truly am free from sin but also how I could live free from any struggle with sin. I'm going to explain that same truth to you, and I want to encourage you with this good news: your struggle with sin doesn't have to define you, entrap you, or last your whole life.

FIND THE WHOLE THOUGHT

It all comes down to context. If you take just the verses that I quoted above, it fully looks like we are trapped in our flesh to an old nature of sin. Paul even says directly that he is sold under sin. But if we read this in context—or in other words, if we read this while keeping in mind what Paul just said in chapter 6—we should naturally have some questions.

After all, in chapter 6 he repeatedly told us we are dead to sin and alive to God, so how could he possibly now say that sin dwells within us? And in chapter 3 he told us that Jesus redeemed us, purchasing us from the sin we had been sold under, so how can he say in chapter 7 that we are still today sold under sin? Only one of these realities can be true. Either we are free from sin because of Jesus, or we are still trapped in sin and sin is still trapped in our flesh.

Whenever we have a question like this, we need to look for more clues, and the first place to look is the very same context. As we do that, consider for a moment that it's pretty rare for us to study three whole chapters at a time (as we will, because we'll include chapter 8 here in just a moment). Three chapters has a lot to say, especially in Romans, and it can be extremely difficult to do justice to that much Scripture in one study or one sermon. For that reason, we don't do it very often. However, Scripture wasn't written in sound bites, a verse here and a verse there. Each New Testament epistle was written as a stream of thought where one thought connects to what comes before and after it. This is especially true for Romans because of the way Paul wrote it.

As we look at the context, first we see chapter 6, which we've talked about already. Chapter 6 says we're so free from sin that we're dead to it. Then we have chapter 7. Interestingly, chapter 7 actually begins with more discussion about how dead to sin we are, using the example of marriage. Verses 1 through 6 talk about how if we are married to someone, we are only married until that person dies. Once they die, we are free to have a relationship with someone else that would have been adultery while our spouse was still alive. In the same way, through Jesus, our relationship to sin died and we are no longer married to it, leaving us free to have relationship with God.

Chapter 7 continues, in verses 7 through 12, to explain the purpose of God's laws about sin, essentially asking how we would have known about sin if God never gave us rules about it. Paul also points out that the laws themselves stirred up even more desire to sin, leading us to sin all the more and drawing us to death.

This is the setup for verses 14 through 24, which I quoted above. As we see it in its place within Paul's stream of thought penned out to the Romans, we discover that his purpose in writing those words was not to excuse a lifelong struggle with sin, but to depict the hopelessness of our ability to conquer sin on our own with only a law to tell us what's wrong. His whole statement in that passage should describe our life before Jesus, not our life after Jesus!

If this wasn't obvious by looking at the context before Romans 7:14–24, it becomes abundantly clear when we look at the beginning of chapter 8:

> There is therefore now no condemnation for those who are in Christ Jesus. For the law of the Spirit of life has set you free in Christ Jesus from the law of sin and death. For God has done what the law, weakened by the flesh, could not do. By sending his own Son in the likeness of sinful flesh and for sin, he condemned sin in the flesh, in order that the righteous requirement of the law might be fulfilled in us, who walk not according to the flesh but according to the Spirit. For those who live according to the flesh set their minds on the things of the flesh, but those who live according to the Spirit set their minds on the things of the Spirit. To set the mind on the flesh is death, but to set the mind on the Spirit is life and peace. For the mind that is set on the flesh is hostile to God, for it does not submit to God's law; indeed, it cannot. Those who are in the flesh cannot please God. *You, however, are not in the flesh but in the Spirit, if in fact the Spirit of God dwells in you.* Anyone who does not have the

Spirit of Christ does not belong to him. But if Christ is in you, although the body is dead because of sin, the Spirit is life because of righteousness. If the Spirit of him who raised Jesus from the dead dwells in you, he who raised Christ Jesus from the dead will also give life to your mortal bodies through his Spirit who dwells in you.—v. 1–11

There is so much here, beginning with Paul's declaration that the law of the Spirit has set us free from the law of sin. That sounds confusing because we don't normally think in those kinds of words, but he had just used those same words to describe the predicament we feel about being trapped in sin. He concluded that passage by saying, "So then, I myself serve the law of God with my mind, but with my flesh I serve the law of sin" (7:25).

Wait. He said, "But with my flesh I serve the law of sin," but then two verses later he said, "For the law of the Spirit of life has set you free in Christ Jesus from the law of sin and death" (8:2)? This means we're getting somewhere because, remember, we are trying to understand whether Paul really means what he said in chapter 6 (that we're free from sin) or whether he meant what he said in chapter 7 (that we're slaves to sin). Apparently, he fully, completely, and truly means we are free from it. This is the work Jesus has accomplished for us, just as Paul already taught us in Romans 3 and 6, telling us we have misunderstood and misapplied Romans 7 anytime we used it to prove we still have a sinful nature.

Paul makes it even clearer as we go on, contrasting those who set their minds on fleshly things and those who set their minds on the Spirit. He finally makes one of his clearest statements on the matter by telling us, "You, however, are not in the flesh but in the Spirit, if in fact the Spirit of God dwells in you" (8:9). Whatever question we might have about what Paul meant in those tricky verses from chapter 7, this clearly tells us he never meant for anyone to think he was telling them their flesh was still alive. He never meant for us to think our old nature still had power over us.

Quite the opposite, he writes to us from two thousand years ago to passionately confirm to us the gospel—that Jesus died for us and that in his death sin completely lost all its power over us. We are completely free from sin and all it brought into our lives—the shame, condemnation, and living death we knew as we struggled with it.

BUT WAIT, THERE'S MORE

If you want to know more from Paul and other writers about how it really is the normal Christian life to live without a daily struggle against sin, a couple of good places to start are Colossians 2:6–3:4 (which is almost like a condensed version of Romans 6–8) and 1 John 2:1, along with the surrounding verses. Ask God to speak to you through these passages. Ultimately, it is his Word, and it's his Spirit who needs to make it alive in you, not my words that somehow convince you this is true.

And, for the sake of clarification, note that I haven't said Christians don't sin at all. We know that isn't true either. Freedom from sin just means we aren't trapped with it in our lives anymore, but we are still free to choose sin if we want to. There's a big difference, though, between a life with occasional failures and a life trapped to the same failure over and over again. A Christian may sin, but they can always immediately gain victory over that sin. A sinner is trapped in their sin, and no matter how hard they try, they are stuck if they never find the Savior.

This is an issue of identity. Are you a Christian, or are you a sinner? Whichever identity you embrace, you will act out of that identity. If you embrace the identity of a sinner, then you will sin by faith, believing that you have no power to overcome. But if you understand the truth that Jesus has already set you completely free from sin, making you his own, and that is your identity, then you will live righteously because of your faith.

Paul tells us this very thing as we continue reading Romans 8. His next words reveal to us the secret of living a life free from the power of sin, and at the heart of it is understanding that we have become something we did not used to be. He tells us that it is by the Spirit we put to death the deeds of the flesh (v. 13). You cannot put the flesh to death by the Spirit if you are white-knuckling your own rule-based righteousness, trying to fulfill every moral obligation you believe God has placed on you. That's exactly what the Jews had done in the Old Testament. It didn't work for them, and it won't work for us today.

Our only hope is Jesus! Thanks to him, we are already set free because he has changed who we are. We are no longer slaves, and we do not have the spirit of slavery that would lead us again into fear. Instead, God has given us his very own Spirit, the Spirit of adoption, who has transformed us from slaves to sons (vv. 15–16). We are God's real and true children, and day by day he is conforming us to his image.

That right there is still the point. He made us to be like him, and he has no sin. His purpose was not just to save us to bring us to heaven, but to save us unto the original purpose for which he made us. If we are still sinners after he saved us, then he didn't really achieve his purpose. But if our salvation truly includes buying us out of slavery to sin (redemption), clearing away all the guilt of sin (justification), and paying for the wrath due because of sin (propitiation), that's a start in the direction of becoming like God again.

We take another step, as not only is the past erased but God also gives us his Spirit. Now we no longer have our history of failure, and we have every possibility for a new future opened to us because of who we have now become—children of God. Think about it. This sounds a lot more like the gospel than a message that tells you to hope for heaven someday, but sorry, you're stuck in sin until then.

This is why it's such a problem when we teach people they are sinners. Satan used Scripture for all three of the recorded temptations he threw at Jesus, and when he tempted Adam and Eve, he started with what God had already said to them. He is more than willing to use passages like "For all have sinned and fall short of the glory of God" to convince people they are hopelessly stuck in sin. He loves to twist God's words and use partial truths to lead us into complete deception. It gets honest, God-fearing people to embrace his lies and live them with passion, believing they come on God's authority. If he can convince us that God says we are sinners, we will say, "Who are we to question God?"

Then, being convinced that God says we're sinners (which implies that he won't help us out of this, because if he didn't save us from it through Jesus, then we're certainly on our own until heaven) but also knowing that God calls us to righteousness, we have fallen into Satan's favorite trap—being convinced we have lack and we are responsible to fill it. This leads us into the belief that we have to follow all God's rules perfectly in order to appease him or make him happy with us. It pressures us to perform, increasing the weight of shame we feel when we fail, and failure is a certainty because we believe we're sinners.

What a downward cycle! We believe we lack righteousness (because we're sinners) and that we need to make up for it (because Jesus won't really give it to us until heaven), so we pressure ourselves and each other to follow all the rules (labor on our own), but we fail, so we feel ashamed, which convinces us all the more that we lack righteousness, and the cycle starts all over again. It drags us down further and further into deeper shame, condemnation, and failure. I know this cycle well. I lived it passionately for nearly ten years with all the zeal for God I had.

But God has given us a real gospel, some truly good news. We are made in his image. Yes, we lost that image, and yes, it's true that nothing we can do could make up for what we lack. But he provided everything we need in Jesus' death and resurrection. Through faith in him we are united with him (Romans 6), completely saved to such a degree that he calls us new creations (2 Corinthians 5:17), filled with his Spirit (Romans 8:15), and set on a course to become like our Father (Romans 8:29).

Our past is irrelevant, our present is opportunity, and our future is unlimited. What remains for us but to change the world?

Chapter 5

BECOMING LIKE GOD

Many words can be used to describe God—righteous, holy, creator, etc.—but one word rises above all the others to describe his personhood—love. It is as we remain in his love, that we enter the process of becoming like him, and if we become like him, it won't be long until love is not just a word that describes God. Soon it will also describe us.

Think of the person you admire most. Let's gather some details. Do you know them personally, or are they perhaps someone you've heard of or studied? Are they a man or a woman? How old are they, or have they already passed away? How much education did they receive? How much money did they make in their lifetime? What was the highest office or position they held?

Wait, I probably started losing you there toward the end, didn't I? Some people do admire high achievers simply because of their achievement and earnings, but for most of you reading this, those last two or three questions started leaving a bad taste in your mouth. You didn't like asking those questions while thinking of someone you highly admire.

This tells us that the reason you admire someone goes beyond their achievement. And even more, it tells us that what you value most for your own life is not achievement. It's not that achievement is bad—after all, most of us want to achieve something with our lives as well; it's just that we want something more. We don't want achievement alone. We were created for this, not just to achieve and exist, but to become something we might simply describe as a person with values.

If we put together a list of the most admired people of recent history, we would find we admire certain characters because we associate them with certain values. When we think of Winston Churchill, we think of integrity. When we think of Martin Luther King Jr., we think of peace or justice. Mother Teresa makes us think of compassion, and Nelson Mandela reminds us of perseverance.

In the same way, if I asked you to tell me one word you associate with God, what would it be? Would you say holy? Righteous? Mighty? Healer? Provider? Would you maybe even say Judge? All of these words do describe God, and some of them are names he even claimed for himself. But there is one word that I believe describes God even above all these. This word is *love*.

Now, the fact that God is love does not alter the fact that he is any of those other words. However, love is different from some of these other words because it is so closely tied to his name, "I Am." We don't say that God is loving, though that is true. And in the same way, we don't say God is righteousness, holiness, mightiness, health, or provision. Love is somehow different from these other words that describe God. It's as though, while these other words describe God, love personifies him. The other words are his attributes, but love is his identity; it's who he is at the very core of his being. It's the center from which all these other attributes find their source. He is holy because he is love. He is righteous because he is love. He heals because he is love. He provides because he is love.

This doesn't put God into a nice little box where we have him all figured out. God does heal because he is love, but that doesn't mean he hates all the sick people in the world. Obviously, there is more mystery to this truth I'm introducing than I have explained here, and more than

There is newness every morning?

BECOMING LIKE GOD

I know how to explain or understand myself, but just consider that to be an invitation to go on that journey with God to figure it out for yourself. I'm not trying to be comprehensive here. I'm simply introducing to you a God whose nature is unquestionably defined by love.

CHOOSING TO TRUST

People have wondered about God's love for a long time. They become offended at the idea that God is loving, and it always comes down to one basic reason. In one form or another, they ask this question, "If God is loving, then why didn't he do something to stop (fill in the blank)?" It could be that they were raped, abused, or had someone die tragically from cancer or a car accident. Or it could be the bigger-picture issues like war, poverty, the Holocaust, or similar events.

Think about this for a moment though. God is love, and he made us to be like him. Through Jesus, he invited all humankind into a process of loving just as he loves. Because of love, he doesn't force this process on anyone. Love is confident and it understands the importance of choice, so it empowers freedom. Control, however, is rooted in insecurity. It says, "I don't trust your choices, so I will control them."

Even in the garden at the beginning, God gave Adam and Eve a choice. He put two trees in the garden so they would have choice, or his love wouldn't have been real love. God knew what their choice would cost him, that it would gruesomely cost him his life, but he preferred that cost to the alternative—abandoning his very nature, which is love. He preferred love over convenience, and genuine relationship over robotic control.

So humankind is free regarding love. We can embrace love himself, joining the process of becoming like him, being conformed to the image of love. Or we can live in our own ways and then try to blame God when bad things happen. Listen, Satan is very crafty in his mission to pervert and degrade you and me, who were made to be like God, to possess what he most desires. Satan knows that to be ultimately successful in his deceptive mission, he has to pervert and degrade how we imagine God to be.

If he can so soil God's reputation among us that we believe evil of God, then he will have accomplished his goal of dragging us more into his image than God's, because then we would no longer see anything marvelous in God that could transform us into something glorious. Simply put, if Satan and his forces can trick us into doubting God's love, then we can no longer be conformed to his love until we learn to renew our minds according to the truth of who God really is.

This means we're going to have to learn to trust God before it feels completely safe to trust him. I know that many of you reading this book have been hurt in ways that made you pull back from God. I won't overlook that pain as though it doesn't matter, because it does matter. At the same time, I know God's love is what we need to be healed of our hurts, set free from our oppressions, and rise above what has imprisoned and held us back in the past.

Whether baby step or bold step, we have to take a step of trusting God to become vulnerable with him so that transformation and healing can happen. We will all be better off if we recognize the opportunity God has given to us, take responsibility for the shortcomings we have had, and embrace a relationship with Love himself. Only he can show us what love is like, and only he can give us what he alone has.

WHERE LOVE BEGINS

What is this process that God has invited us into that conforms us to his love? God made you to be like him, and he is love, so how does this transformation happen in your life and my life? John writes the answer for us:

> Whoever confesses that Jesus is the Son of God, God abides in him, and he in God. So we have come to know and to believe the love that God has for us. God is love, and whoever abides in love abides in God, and God abides in him. By this is love perfected

with us, so that we may have confidence for the day of judgment, because as he is so also are we in this world. There is no fear in love, but perfect love casts out fear. For fear has to do with punishment, and whoever fears has not been perfected in love. We love because he first loved us.—1 John 4:15–19

Let's take a look at this from the bottom, where we see that John gives us a foundational principle: we love because he first loved us.

I've been in ministry more than half my life, and one thing I've noticed is that people generally don't understand the basic principles of resources. Simply put, to give something away, you have to get it from somewhere. Because financial credit is so easy to get, many people don't even understand this principle when it comes to money, but let's imagine ourselves living in the time when you actually paid for things with real currency made from gold and silver. Let's go back to the time when business deals were made according to the weight of the money you had, not according to currency with an artificially declared value.

In those days, if you didn't have the gold, silver, cattle, sheep, goats, servants, slaves, or some other form of wealth, you couldn't buy anything. No matter how long you stood in the market and told the sellers you wanted their product, no one would give you anything because you didn't have any money with you to buy it. You had to possess something before you could give it away or use it.

While it seems that some people are coming around to the fact that you have to have money before you can spend any, many of these same people don't understand how this principle works with other forms of resources. If I have booked my schedule full, I am not able to give a hurting family from my church any of my time. If I expend all my energy working my job, I have none left for my family and friends. You get the point.

Love is similar to this because it's a resource, but it is different from other resources like time or energy because there is only one true source of love—God. We love because he first loved us. The reason we have love to give is limited to only one thing—God loved us first.

Now, God's love can be difficult to trace. For most of us, our first memory of feeling loved wasn't because of an encounter we had with God. Our first notion of loving someone else probably didn't wait for that kind of encounter either. Instead, we learned to love because we had family to love us. I know not everyone enjoyed this blessing, but many have and it still holds true that most of us first learned to love because of family.

There is no contradiction here between us receiving love from family and us receiving love from God. It's like how we don't receive our money directly from our nation's treasury but from our employer. Eventually, however, you would trace back every dollar, dime, and penny back to the US Treasury, or at least to a mint where it was stamped or printed. In the same way, all love originates from God. He is the ultimate source. His love has trickled down through generation after generation, through friendships and relationships, from one kind gesture to another, where love he first expressed at some point in the past to a person has now found its way to you or me. The person who gave us the love isn't the source of their own love. They got it from somewhere, and eventually that somewhere is Jesus.

WHY WE LOVE

When we understand that God is the source of all the love we have ever experienced, we need to let that understanding really sink in. Like countless others, I learned the song "Jesus Loves Me" in Sunday school as a child. I learned the gospel and was told God loves me. I memorized John 3:16: "For God so loved the world …"

I know God loves me, but do I really? Is my heart confident of God's love as a present reality in my life? If I picture God, can I get past the airbrushed Jesus paintings to see what he's really like? Or if I picture God and I'm honest, do I picture someone stiff and emotionally distant, like the statue of Abraham Lincoln at the Lincoln Memorial? Do I picture him as an angry father so I walk on eggshells around him and live my life as a performance in hopes he won't fly off the handle at me? Can I get past all these pictures to see a face in God that smiles at me, laughs with me, cries with me, and holds me close?

If I will take the time to let every experience of love I have ever received sink in so I know that I know that I know that it all came from God, I will begin to see his face this way, and so will you. But I have to take the time. I have to stop, to not just run past those happy moments of my life. I have to pause, let them sink in, and receive them as kisses from a good father who loves me. This is what enables me to love. This is the filling station where I become whole and complete, sufficient within myself, because of God, to love fully even as I have been fully loved.

Where I grew up, I was taught that I needed to love people. Now, when God grabbed ahold of my life, he really did a number on me. I was absolutely sold out. I sang "Jesus Freak" by DC Talk with all my heart and soul. I wore Christian T-shirts to school five days a week. I had my assortment of cross necklaces and my purity ring. I was a good church boy, and I did everything I could to do all I was supposed to do.

As a young fifteen-year-old, I sat in the front row at a fall retreat and listened as the guest speaker told us that we were all missionaries whether we knew it or not. God was calling us to reach somewhere, and each of us was going to ask God where that place was. I did what I was told. I asked God. He told me my high school was my mission field.

I protested. I told God that I was just a freshman and I knew my place in the pecking order. I knew that in my seniority-minded school, I was lower than pond scum. To make it worse, I was homeschooled from first through eighth grade and didn't know anyone in my school. I had no friends, no influence, and no connections. I was the last person qualified to reach my school for Jesus, and I told God I thought so. But God told me he'd chosen me anyway.

So again I obeyed, but I didn't know how to obey. How do you reach a school for Jesus anyway? I asked God—repeatedly—over the course of that freshman year and in the years that followed. God only ever gave me one answer. Actually, he only ever gave me one word. That word was *love*. God told me that love would reach my high school for him.

Again, I obeyed. I did what I was told to do. I did my best to love however I could imagine it looked. I hung out with the least popular people by choice. I counseled and ministered to the down-and-out girls who struggled with depression and cutting (and learned a lot about what not to do in ministry and how to keep healthy boundaries!). I shared the gospel everywhere I could, organized and led my school Bible study for three years, organized See You at the Pole three of those years, wore WWJD bracelets and hung them on my backpack, prayed on my knees at my locker before school every day, led prayer circles before some of my choir concerts, and tried anything else you could possibly think of to try to love the people around me and lead them to Jesus.

I worked hard at love, but I never learned during those years how to receive God's love for myself. I labored and did all I knew to do—all I thought I was supposed to do—but I didn't have much to give because I didn't know how to start with receiving. I didn't know how to love *because* I was first loved.

Only when we begin by learning to receive love can we go out to love others and have it be natural, not forced, and powerful.

HOW TO KNOW GOD'S LOVE

Our ability to love others begins with our ability to receive God's love, so how do we receive God's love? We can look a little farther back in the passage from 1 John to find our answer: "Whoever confesses that Jesus is the Son of God, God abides in him, and he in God. So we have come to know and to believe the love that God has for us" (4:15–16). This verse makes God's love so incredibly easy. Start halfway through, where it says, "So we have come to know and to believe the love that God has for us." Read that again slowly, one word at a time, and let it sink in:

So. This means "in this way" or "this is how." In other words, this single word tells us we have a prescribed, promised way by which we can be sure of God's love in our lives. What a small but powerful word! No matter the shame you carry, no matter your past, you have a promised pathway to being completely sure of knowing God's love. That has to make you feel good!

We. You and me, all of us, every human that could possibly be included in "we" can take hold of the truth in this verse because of this one powerful word.

Have come. This is a past-tense statement, which means it's something that is intended for our past, not our future. God's love is not some promised experience for a heavenly future. God intends it for us right now!

To know. These words mean experiential knowledge and are used in other contexts to indicate sexual intimacy. Sexual intimacy is what God created to cause husband and wife to become one flesh, so this kind of knowing really is deeply experiential and unquestionably real. It is not a knowledge you gain just by learning something, but by living it. It is never theoretical knowledge where we think we know something but is always a knowledge we are completely certain of.

And believe. Knowing God's love alone is wonderful, but it's not enough. We don't just know God's love, even as intimate as that knowing is. We also believe God's love. How many of us know for certain that God loves us but still have a hard time believing it when we have just messed up? Well, not anymore, because now we have a promised way to both know and believe God's love.

The love God has. This is just ridiculous. I mean, God is love, but he also has love. When I consider that God is completely infinite beyond all we can comprehend, and then add that he is love, and then understand that he has love, what I imagine are storehouses larger than solar systems filled with love. I picture endless supplies, limitless resources, unending provision of love, because it continually flows from his infiniteness whenever it is spent.

For us. Why has God stored up infinite resources of love? Who is it for? It is for you and me. We are the object of his affection. Worthy or not, here it comes.

If you were to paraphrase this incredible sentence John wrote here

BECOME YOU

for us, it might say, "This is how everyone throughout history—including you and me—have already before this moment come to taste, touch, see, feel, and become saturated in the unending, limitless, perfect love that the infinite creator God has for you and me to such a powerfully deep extent that we actually believe this love truly belongs to us."

So how do we come to know and believe the love God has for us? We look to what comes right before "so," where it says, "Whoever confesses that Jesus is the Son of God, God abides in him, and he in God" (1 John 4:15). That's how.

I know. You're probably wondering how these two verses are even connected, but don't move on too quickly, because this is the part that shows us just how incredibly simple God's powerful love is.

Let's start our discussion of this by taking a quick poll. If you have confessed that Jesus is the Son of God, please raise your hand. Okay, I'm assuming that probably everyone reading this book just raised their hand, or would have if this were a legitimate poll. If I asked you whether Jesus is the Son of God, you would say yes. Of course you would, because you're a Christian, right? Okay, so now that we have the first part of this verse covered, we know that what comes next applies to all of us.

If you believe Jesus is the Son of God, God abides in you and you abide in God. A few years ago, my middle child had a habit of asking, when we were out driving somewhere, whether we were going home. Eventually, of course, we would always be heading home and would tell him, "Yes, we are going home." Every time, he would protest, "No! I don't want to go home!" We would tell him that we have to go home because that is where we live.

We always eventually returned home because that is where we live—it's where we abide. Well, if you confess that Jesus is the Son of God, God abides in you and you abide in God. You are where he lives and he is where you live. It wouldn't matter if you somehow left for a while; you would come back because he is where you live. Where else would you go? Where else could you possibly go? He is where you live. And even if you somehow left, you are still where he lives, and he isn't leaving you!

This means that the constant reality of your life is that you are united with God. You live in him and he lives in you. You have constant fellowship with him. He isn't far off. He's more intimate with you than our words can even express.

But pay attention to how all this happened, because you didn't really need to do anything for it. All you or I needed to do was confess that Jesus is the Son of God, then all these other things began to happen. Suddenly we abide in God and he abides in us, and then simply through that abiding we come to know and believe the love God has for us.

THE PROCESS OF PERFECT LOVE

It's almost as though John could see our confusion at this point, because it's natural to wonder how this equates so perfectly. If we drew it out like a math problem, it helps us see more clearly what John is saying so far. Confess Jesus is God's Son = God abides in us and we abide in God = We know and believe God's love. We can see clearly what he's saying, but we might well wonder how all that can be true, because few, if any, of us have experienced that.

John anticipated this confusion, so he wrote the next verse to help us understand that he's introducing us to a process, not an instantaneous transformation. He writes:

> God is love, and whoever abides in love abides in God, and God abides in him. By this is love perfected with us, so that we may have confidence in the day of judgment, because as he is so also are we in this world. There is no fear in love, but perfect love casts out fear. For fear has to do with punishment, and whoever fears has not been perfected in love.—1 John 4:16–18

The first words here drop a bomb that changes everything: *God is love.* God is love. This one simple truth is about to turn our world upside down. Put it into the context of everything we already know. We confess

Jesus, meaning we abide in God, but God is love and when we understand the most basic, primary nature of the one in whom we live and of the one who lives in us, we begin to change inside.

Take a moment right now to simply say this over yourself a few times: "God lives in me; love lives in me. I live in God; I live in love." Now, hold onto this truth and don't change the subject for the rest of your life. Don't let your experience of your own choices or what others do to you lower what you know to be true about yourself. You live in God and he lives in you. You live in love and love lives in you. Let this truth wash over you day after day, week after week, year after year. Set up your home in this truth and never move. Abide in love!

I think there are too many Christians who think so little of themselves that they almost apologize to Jesus because he died for them. If they were honest, they might pray like this, "Jesus, I receive your salvation, but really, you shouldn't have done that for me. I'm not worth it." Then they live as though they're afraid Jesus will discover they really aren't worth the price he paid for them. They avoid him because they think his presence reminds him of their shame. If we treat him this way, then we don't understand the nature of his love.

Listen, don't confess Jesus as the Son of God but then run away from his embrace. If you come to God for salvation, stay near to him the rest of your life so you can become like him! Realize that receiving him meant receiving his indelible love.

No, you can't earn God's love, but yes, you are worthy of it. I'll say it again: you are worthy of God's love. How can I be so confident in saying that? Because God himself said he loves you! How could I say that you aren't worthy of his love when he obviously thinks you are? Whether you feel worthy or not has nothing to do with it; receive his love anyway. Receive the truth that the price has been willingly paid, he considered you worthy of it, and he gave the sacrifice, fully intending to make you a living home for his love forever.

When we simply receive the truth that God has made us the object of his love, really and truly, and that we can live in his love continually just by belonging to him, it begins a process John describes with the words, "By this is love perfected in us" (1 John 4:17).

Wow. I mean, seriously, who wouldn't want to have love perfected in them, to know they are perfectly loved and that they also perfectly love? This is the result of the process John is telling us about. It's the process that started when we confessed Jesus as the Son of God. When we did that, it directly led to us abiding in God and him abiding in us. And since God is love, we can also abide in love simply by recognizing that this is the core nature of the God who has become our home. So when we confess Jesus, we abide in God, and God is love, so we abide in love, which leads to love becoming perfect with us.

Perfected—that's the word John uses. Perfected! Nothing lacking! No chips, dents, scratches, or rust! Perfect in love! That's what's in store for you and me when we simply abide in God, knowing that he is love itself.

There are so many benefits to this, and John specifically tells us that fearlessness is chief among them. Perfect love casts out fear. It drives it right out, proving to us in the depths of our soul that we have escaped punishment of any kind. What is there to be ashamed of anymore? We are loved! In fact, we are loved right out of any condemning predicament we earned. We are loved right out of the consequences for all our mistakes and foolish choices. We are loved to such a confidence in God that our confidence has become bigger than our dread of consequence. Confidence has overcome the dread until it is gone and only confidence remains.

And did you notice that, right in the heart of these verses, John reminds us of how this all ties in to God's intent from the beginning—that as he is, so also are we *in this world*. We aren't waiting for heaven for this to happen; it's happening right now. We're not waiting for a new earth; it's happening in this one. It's a process that started when we confessed Jesus is the Son of God, but it's not stopping until we are fearless, perfected in love, and made just like God so that as he is, so also are we in this world.

All this leads us back to where we began: we love because he first loved us. He loved us so much that he gave his only Son to die for us so that we could live. His love began the process that we joined by confessing that it's all true. We believed, and that faith signed us up for the journey of becoming like God, which means being perfected in love.

Of course becoming like God would have to mean being perfected in love. After all, that's who he is.

Chapter 6

DIVINE CONTRADICTION

You can't become who God made you to be without loving yourself. But you also can't become who God made you to be without serving others' dreams before your own. While these two truths may seem to contradict each other, learning to walk the balance between them is one of the most important lessons we need to learn in order to become ourselves.

The walls were light blue, a little grayer and more pale than the sky. Fluorescent bulbs cast their harsh light through the room. The air continually smelled damp, as this room was dug deep into a hillside, serving as both basement and backdoor to the strip mall upstairs. Often during the day, a repeated, fast-paced pounding would sound from above, occasionally broken up by a louder *thud-thud* on the ceiling.

I have so many good memories from this less than romantic room. It was the prayer room for the church I worked for, The House Church, and we happened to be right beneath a small fitness center. I don't know if they ever heard our loud worship music, but I know we heard every jogger on the treadmill and every weight that was dropped.

It was in the office of that prayer room, sitting at a folding table we used as a conference table, where God gave me one of the first (and foundational) lessons of my journey to become me. He took me to a famous passage for young pastors, 1 Timothy 4, and began to walk me through it. I started in verse 12: "Let no one despise you for your youth, but set the believers an example in speech, in conduct, in love, in faith, in purity."

The context for this adds meaning and depth to these words. Paul wrote the book we call 1 Timothy as a letter to his young spiritual son, Timothy. We read in the book of Acts about how Paul met Timothy in his travels, led him to Jesus, and began to disciple him. Perhaps more than anyone else, Timothy became Paul's primary disciple and spiritual son. For that reason, we also see several times when Paul needed to follow up with a church he planted but could not go for one reason or another and sent Timothy in his place.

Paul sent this letter to Timothy in the midst of just such an assignment. Paul had planted a church in Ephesus and had sent Timothy to oversee it, teaching and training there while also establishing leadership within the church. There was only one problem: Timothy was a young man and not long established in either life or ministry. No one questioned Paul's authority in that church. He was a well-established man who had accomplished much academically and in ministry. His resume was long and significant. But Timothy had none of that. All he had was a renowned apostle who believed in him.

So here was Timothy, a young man in an established church in real need of some leadership and direction. He may have never done anything like this before, though he had tagged along with Paul when Paul did it. But now Paul wasn't there. He was alone. How did he know what to do? He starts with the basics:

Don't let anyone look down on him because of his age. Thankfully, Paul didn't stop there, because if he had then we could interpret this verse very differently. We might see this as an instruction to shake his fist at those who despised his inexperience, as empowerment to confront them and put them in their place. But it's not that at all, and we know it's not that because Paul immediately tells Timothy how to prevent people from looking down on his youth.

The key to Timothy's ability to lead people older than him rested in how he lived his life. Paul charged him to become an example to the believers in five areas: in the words he spoke, in the way he lived, in the fervor of his love, in the sincerity of his faith, and in the integrity of his heart. If he managed his own life in this way, it would prove to any potential detractors that he had what it takes to lead a church well.

What does it tell us that Timothy's response to those who looked down on him had nothing to do with them and everything to do with him? Well, it tells us a lot about how leadership is all about taking responsibility and very little about gaining positions and titles, but that's a subject for another day. More to the point of this book, it gives us a window into how to balance two of the most important truths we learn as we become who God made us to be.

INTRODUCING A CONTRADICTION

The two truths we need to learn are these: we need to love ourselves, and we need to serve others wholeheartedly. In reality, these don't actually contradict each other, but like Paul's statement to Timothy, they can appear to contradict each other at first glance.

It would be easy to think loving yourself looks like dedicating your life to the pursuit of your identity—to doing your own thing. When someone calls you to help with something that feels outside of who God has said you are, you stay focused on the goal and turn down the opportunity to serve. You can put a lot of different buzzwords to this—building your platform, getting your name out, establishing a reputation—and they can be good in the right season, but this isn't the primary way to love yourself and build your identity.

Here's why that can't be the main way you build your identity: if you build your identity by focusing on yourself, then your identity will be hollow and self-made instead of powerful and God made. The plain fact of the matter is that the tool God uses to craft our identity is the crucible of service and sacrifice. If we aren't willing to lay everything down for someone else to promote them, God can look at our lives and recognize that we would not use the promotion he'd give us to serve others. We would only use our elevated status to serve ourselves, and that's not the purpose of a title, position, or platform. Selfish gain can't build the kingdom of God and it won't be rewarded by God in heaven.

So what's a person supposed to do? How do you ever get to your own identity and purpose if you are always serving someone else's? How do you fulfill your dreams if you are always serving another person's dreams? A huge part of the answer to these questions is simply that you need to have faith that God will be true to his words over your life. But let's dig deeper than that, because we do find a lot of helpful clarity when we understand what it means to love ourselves and to serve others.

WHY DISAGREE WITH GOD?

Everyone knows we're supposed to love others. If that's not a foundational teaching of Christianity, then it's the very first lesson in how to apply our faith once we believe in Jesus. After all, it's right there in Scripture for us where God tells us that all his rules are summed up in one simple statement: love him with all our heart, soul, mind, and strength, and love our neighbor as ourselves (Matthew 22:37; Luke 10:27).

Many people know God commands us to love, but unfortunately it seems that few have seen the condition God placed on that command, saying to love your neighbor "as you love yourself." If you don't love yourself, it will be difficult to love your neighbor. That's why I can say with perfect confidence that God wants you to love yourself! He loves you, so loving yourself is simply agreeing with how he feels, thinks, and acts toward you.

In the conversation Jesus had with his disciples in the upper room before he died, Jesus commanded them to love one another three different times:

DIVINE CONTRADICTION

"A new commandment I give to you, that you love one another, *even as I have loved you*, that you also love one another. By this all men will know that you are my disciples, if you have love for one another."— John 13:34–35

"My Father is glorified in this, that you bear much fruit, and so prove to be my disciples. *Just as the Father has loved me, I have also loved you; abide in my love.* If you keep my commandments, you will abide in my love; just as I have kept my Father's commandments and abide in His love. These things I have spoken to you so that my joy may be in you, and that your joy may be made full. This is my commandment, that you love one another, *just as I have loved you.* ... You are my friends if you do what I command you."—John 15:8–14

"This I command you, that you love one another."— John 15:17

Three times in one conversation, Jesus repeats himself: "This is my commandment, that you love one another." It's really hard to miss that point when you take it in context, but so often we read these verses either apart from context or through lenses that bring extra meaning that changes what Jesus was saying.

But we can't miss something else Jesus says three times in this conversation: "I have loved you." His love expressed toward them is clearly the foundation of their love expressed toward one another. Jesus' love for them began with the Father's love for him, then their love for each other began with his love for them. As I said before, love always comes from a source, and the Father is the ultimate source of all love.

I already covered how to walk through this process, how this really defines the Christian life of becoming like God. God is love, and as we receive his love it transforms us into his love for the rest of the world. So while there's plenty more I could say about that from these passages, that isn't my point here. My point is simply to state that if God loves us, it is good for us to agree with him by loving ourselves as well. When we begin to love ourselves, then and only then will we be able to genuinely love the people around us. If there is ever a situation where you recognize that you lack the love required to thrive in that place, your grit and determination cannot help you unless they drive you into God's heart to find deeper, richer resources of love that then compel you to right actions in your circumstances. You don't need willpower, you need transformation!

As God's love saturates you, you will start to love the world around you more, but you will also love yourself more. The question I want to answer here is how to live that righteous self-love. What does it look like to love yourself?

WHAT SELF-LOVE LOOKS LIKE

Self-love, most often, looks like the ability to establish boundaries and say no. Life is filled with opportunities to help, serve, pitch in, meet, visit, get involved, and become absolutely, incredibly overbusy with all sorts of good activities. But too much of a good thing can quickly become a bad thing.

I've mentioned researcher Brené Brown before. This is another area where her studies help us; in her search for how to cultivate wholehearted living, she discovered an interesting and apparent paradox. She found that the most compassionate people were also the ones with the best personal boundaries.[4] This surprised her, but she says it seems their ability to give a meaningful no is what created opportunities for them to also sometimes give a powerful yes when someone asked for help.

So many of us, in the interest of compassion and helping as many people as we can, spread ourselves so thin that we're of no substantial good to anyone or anything, often including our families. For my family, this means we have already drawn some predetermined boundaries for our children.

With five children, we don't think it's possible to let each child get involved in sports and still have a healthy, family-centered culture in our home. We've simply seen too many large families trying to run two parents to three or more places five nights a week, sometimes nearly year-round. Dinners are rushed, time together is too often just in a car, and more time is spent with coaches and friends than with each other. Because of the values my wife and I have for family, and because we want to pass those values on to our children, we simply have a boundary that our kids won't get deeply involved in sports. (Note, I'm describing my values here, not prescribing what yours should be.)

I know other families that just don't do sleepovers. Many ministers I know won't ride alone in a vehicle with someone of the opposite sex or meet one on one with them behind closed doors. It limits their opportunities to minister, but it protects them from potentially bad situations.

One of the people I know who is best at drawing boundaries is the primary leader I've followed for the last ten years, Jamey VanGelder. One example from this in the early days after he planted The House Church is that everyone knew Monday was his family day. It didn't matter who tried to call him or how many times they called, he was unreachable on his family day.

These are all just examples of boundaries, but the point is, you need boundaries. You have to protect life for yourself so you have something to give away to others. Just as God first placed Adam and Eve in an enclosed garden before commanding them to cultivate and keep it, each of us needs an enclosed place where life can thrive. If we let our boundaries get overrun, then we have no garden left. All the people in our life dictate how we cultivate our garden and then we wonder why we always feel stressed and full of turmoil.

Self-love certainly looks like boundaries. It can also look like wisdom. Self-love gets a job and learns financial responsibility, because let me tell you, there isn't much worse than always having the financial institutions in your life telling you what you need to do with your money because you owe them more than you can pay. Self-love recognizes the core relationships in your life and invests in them, separating them from relationships that aren't as important. Self-love honors governing authorities, because they do have authority over you and can make you suffer if you dishonor them. Self-love looks to invest toward the future, not devouring all your resources today.

Self-love can be a lot of things, but what I have found most people need to hear is that self-love is God's plan for you, and it's good. They need to hear that self-love draws boundaries and they don't need to always say yes to every chance they get to help or serve someone. Yes, I know service is important in the kingdom of God, and we're about to talk about that half of this coin, but if you serve so much that you bankrupt yourself and have a breakdown, that helps no one, least of all yourself.[5]

FAITHFUL STEWARDSHIP

But you can't always say no to opportunities to serve. And if you don't have people asking you to help with things, chances are pretty good that you've somehow communicated you aren't interested in helping and you need to start looking for ways to help. The question isn't *whether* you should serve and help those around you, but *how* you should serve and help others. What I'm about to tell you will provide some guidelines that can perhaps give focus to where and how you serve, and what you can hope will grow from your service.

Jesus was constantly teaching his disciples how to thrive in his kingdom. He would often use financial principles to illustrate his point, incorporating things from the seen world to help them understand how the unseen works. In one such teaching, Jesus told them, "If you have not been faithful in that which is another's, who will give you that which is your own?" (Luke 16:12). This is one small sentence that carries such a big impact. In this we see a principle God uses to determine who actually gets to live out their own dreams, anointed and blessed by him to take them beyond all we could have imagined. He is telling us that service is the pathway to gaining our own destiny.

We can find examples of this throughout Scripture, where one generation's identity is tied to that of the generation before it so that without one the other won't become fulfilled. This is called a generational mindset.

The first time we see it in Scripture comes when God gives a promise to Abraham that his descendants would number as the stars in the heavens or the sand on the shore. Abraham had only one son who inherited that promise (Isaac), and although Isaac had two sons, only one of them also inherited the promise (Jacob). This promise was so large that it took generations to grow. The first generation had one son, the second had two sons, but the third generation had twelve sons. Finally, Jacob became Israel, and God gave him the breakthrough his father and grandfather had believed God would give them. Those twelve sons each became tribes of God's chosen nation.

Hundreds of years later, during another major shift in Israel's history, David desired to do something magnificent for God by building a temple for him so he no longer had to dwell in a tent, but God told him his son would complete that work. David didn't receive those words, toss up his hands, and do nothing. Instead, he poured himself into Solomon and saved up all the resources his son would need to build the temple. Solomon was then able to begin his crowning work just three years into his reign because of the inheritance David left for him. This was a multigenerational work of identity that shaped history.

Again, many generations later, we have another example in Elijah and Elisha. Elijah was a renowned prophet who did powerful signs and wonders. One of the less notable things about him, however, is that during his time there were bands of prophets in many cities, known as the sons of the prophets. (Samuel started these groups and they still existed in Elijah's day.) While all these other people were known as prophets, Elisha was simply known as Elijah's servant. Nevertheless, only Elisha had the faithfulness to follow Elijah out into the wilderness and receive from him a double portion of what God had given Elijah. See clearly what happened there, because it perfectly follows what Jesus gave as our pattern. There were many prophets serving God in Israel, but there was only one servant to Elijah. Elisha had no notoriety as a prophet and was only known as a servant, yet it was exactly that service that led to his promotion into the double portion.

Elisha then went on to his own ministry, and Scripture records double the miracles from Elisha's ministry as it records from Elijah's. Elisha also had servants, but all of them failed various tests of character or faith to be able to inherit what God had given Elisha, so he died with God's anointing still on him. The power of God remained on him so strongly, even after death, that when a dead body from battle was thrown into his grave, the body came back to life after touching Elisha's bones (2 Kings 13:20–21).

The New Testament has its own examples of this, as the disciples left everything for three and a half years to follow Jesus before entering into their own purpose in life. Similarly, Paul served in ambiguity for fourteen years before following Barnabas into the nations and eventually becoming the great man we remember him to be today. Paul also had his own disciple, Timothy, who was possibly Paul's most faithful servant. It was in Timothy's service to Paul that he found his own identity and purpose.

Over and over again we see this example in Scripture, that what qualifies someone to be given something of their own is to faithfully serve someone else. This is a value in the kingdom of God—you become promoted not through putting yourself forward, but through putting yourself at the bottom. This is even the basis for our reward in heaven, as Jesus tells us that faithful stewardship of what he has given us here is what builds for us a heavenly reward.

WHY WE SERVE

Honestly, it's fairly easy to see why God organizes his kingdom this way. It goes right back to the very theme of this book—that God made you to be like him. God serves, and when we become like him we will also serve. As God recognizes that we have grown more into his image than we used to be, he rewards that growth with greater opportunities. In our eyes, those opportunities can look like a promotion, a greater platform, bigger influence, more favor, and those sorts of things, but not always.

This is exactly what Jesus tried to explain to his disciples when they argued over who was the greatest. He said:

> "You know that the rulers of the Gentiles lord it over them, and their great ones exercise authority over them. It shall not be so among you. But whoever would be great among you must be your servant, and whoever would be first among you must be your slave, even as the Son of Man came not to be served but to serve, and to give his life as a ransom for many."—Matthew 20:25–28

Jesus didn't point his disciples at some rule they needed to follow or some law Moses required them to obey. He simply said, "Look, you've seen what I do. I came to serve and give my life for you. Do that for one another." The sacrificial service Jesus demonstrated is the very sort of action that founded the kingdom of God. How can we build on that foundation except by following his example by serving others?

There are two levels of service Jesus offers to us here. The first one is a group of people he describes as servants. The Greek word here (*diakonos*) indicates those who follow the commands of another, literally the servant of a king or someone who waited on tables.[6]

This is the kind of servant the apostles looked for in the early days of the church when Greek widow believers were being overlooked in the distribution of food (Acts 6). The seven men who were chosen to serve in this way did an important job, but it was a side job; it didn't require them to make much sacrifice to do what they were called to do. The important part is that they were willing to give that sacrifice and fulfilled their duty faithfully. This simple act of service seems to have been significant enough to have earned them mention in the Bible, and, more to the point, a mention in the Bible because their service qualified them to be seen as great among the believers. Service made them great in the kingdom, and it can make us great in the kingdom too. This is a level of service I believe all Christians are called to give.

There is another level Jesus presents to us, however, that I believe some are required to give in order to really fulfill their created purpose. It could be that God wants all of us to walk through this level of service, but I honestly don't know for sure because it is so extreme. It is the example Jesus gave us, as you'll soon see, and it's the example many other fathers and mothers of faith gave us, but I'm not sure it's an example that's required of all of us. This level of service is to truly lay your life down for another, to become a slave.

Slave is a harsh word, and looking into the Greek doesn't lighten it any. The word Jesus used is sometimes translated "bondslave," and it is a powerful picture for us today. A bondslave was someone who had been a slave but had either served their time (this was sometimes done to repay debts, for example) or in some other way earned their freedom, yet instead of leaving their master they chose to intentionally forsake freedom and continue to serve their master out of love. As a sign of this commitment, the master would drive a stake through the servant's ear and pierce it, permanently marking them as a bondslave who then belonged to that master for life.

Here's the crazy part, though, so hold on to your hat. Jesus didn't say that whoever would be greatest among us must become *his* slave; he said whoever would be greatest among us must become *your* slave. When you look at this in context, you have to understand that Jesus was talking about how he wanted his disciples to serve each other. He was setting the bar for what excellence looks like in the kingdom of God, and he wanted them to know that serving him was barely Service 101. The design is actually for us to become like him in his service to such an extent that we give our lives for one another.

Obviously, this means something more than service projects, feeding the poor on occasion, or being an usher at church. To me, this looks like a friend of mine (who I'm sure would prefer for me to not name him) who almost completed his doctorate and could teach as a professor in college or pastor any church, drawing a nice salary to keep life comfortable, but instead chooses to minister every day in a small church in one of the worst parts of downtown Minneapolis with no salary or guarantee of income. He sings for drug addicts and refugees, drawing them into encounters with Jesus that set them free. He gives his life, not just for

Jesus, but for these lost and forgotten people who have been cast out from society.

I don't know what that kind of service looks like in your life, but God can tell you. If you ask to be truly great in his kingdom, it will require this kind of service, service that truly lays down your life for another—either for a person (like Elisha for Elijah, leading to his inheriting Elijah's mantle) or for a group of people (like many of the prophets or my friend).

GOD'S PATHWAY TO PROMOTION

So I ask again, how can you possibly lay your life down as a bondslave to someone else without also laying down your identity and losing who God made you to be? How is it possible, even in God's kingdom, for that to be the path for you to find and fulfill who you were born to become?

We only need to look at Jesus to find the answer in his example. Paul wrote it best in these words to the Philippians:

> Have this mind among yourselves, which is yours in Christ Jesus, who, though he was in the form of God, did not count equality with God a thing to be grasped, but emptied himself, by taking the form of a servant, being born in the likeness of men. And being found in human form, he humbled himself by becoming obedient to the point of death, even death on a cross. *Therefore God has highly exalted him and bestowed on him the name that I above every name*, so that at the name of Jesus every knee should bow, in heaven and on earth and under the earth, and every tongue confess that Jesus Christ is Lord, to the glory of God the Father.—Philippians 2:5–11

Jesus perfectly showed us what God is like in the very act of humbling himself to take on human form and die on a cross. He laid his life down for us. He came not to be served, but to serve and to give his life as a ransom. Yet it was because of that very act of becoming our bondslave that he was elevated by the Father above every being in all creation. His service led to his promotion. His humility led to his exaltation. His sacrifice led to his blessing.

This exaltation was one he couldn't have achieved without his debasement. If he had never gone low, he would have never been lifted high. And he had the chance to take a shortcut, to cheat his way into something that would have resembled his God-given identity and purpose. Satan offered him the whole world, to make him king of all creation, if only he would bow before him.

Jesus could have had a similar promotion to the one his Father offered him without the suffering, without laying his life down for us, without becoming our bondslave, but that shortcut would have also cut short his identity. The only way for Jesus to become who he was born of a virgin to be was to go all the way through the suffering and humiliation that was part of his service to humankind.

I don't know what service might be required for you to fulfill your identity, but I know service will be required. And I know that loving yourself truly means being willing to go through it, to embrace it, and to be faithful with it until you can say like Jesus, "It is finished." What does that mean? What will that take? Who is involved in that? Only God can fill in those details for you.

But just like so much of the process of becoming you, try not to spend too long looking at the cost. It was the joy set before him that enabled Jesus to endure the cross, despising its shame (Hebrews 12:2). Look to the joy of the promotion that's coming. Look to the glory of the identity God has called you to become. Embrace those things even as you embrace the serving.

And don't forget, this isn't a rule. And if it becomes a rule for you because you read it here, it won't have life in it. But if it becomes part of your new nature in Christ Jesus that you have because you first saw it in him, then it will be the most natural thing for you to do. It won't be a fight or a struggle, even if it's painful and costly.

SERVE AS YOU

So here's the bottom line of this apparent contradiction: love yourself enough to draw boundaries that enable you to serve someone else. Then, when humility leads to exaltation (because it does, see Matthew 23:12), embrace the promotion and use your elevated position to serve even more.

Your identity isn't for you—Jesus is on the throne yet he lives in constant intercession for us—so whatever position or identity God gives you is for the purpose of serving, not because that's your obligation but because in him that has become your heart just as it is his heart. If you don't want to serve, then run away from God, because if you run to him, you'll become like him and if you become like him, then you'll serve because he is constantly serving people who don't deserve it. But some serve by scrubbing toilets or changing diapers and some serve by running companies or governments that change the world. Some serve by administrating details privately where no one will see their service, and some serve by publicly making movies or music that shape the way we think.

I'll sign off on this chapter by telling you about Luke—Dr. Luke. Dr. Luke wrote two books of the New Testament, yet we have no record of him doing any ministry of his own of any kind. He wrote the gospel of Luke, the one chosen by the makers of *The Jesus Film* to use as their script, and now that film has been viewed over five billion times, translated into more than a thousand languages, seen in every nation of the world, and led to more than two hundred million people deciding to follow Jesus.[7] Luke's version of the Christmas story is quoted by Linus in *The Charlie Brown Christmas Special*. And, of course, it's one of the only four gospels chosen to be immortalized in Scripture, touching an untold number of lives through two millennia and counting since it was written.

Dr. Luke also wrote the book of Acts. He wrote it from firsthand knowledge he gained as he simply followed Paul around to chronicle his journeys. Without Luke's faithful pen, we would know nothing about the early church except for what tradition told us. We would have no understanding of our roots, of the miracles done in those days, or of the explosive, world-changing power the gospel had everywhere it went.

I wonder how many people thought to or actually did pressure Luke to minister for himself. I wonder if anyone told him that being a doctor was unspiritual because they believed going to doctors meant a lack of faith in God's power to heal. I wonder if anyone said, "You've spent all that time with Paul. Why don't you do some ministry yourself?" In short, I wonder how many people pressured Luke to become someone God didn't make him to be, to serve in a way that was contrary to his purpose.

I'm sure glad Luke loved himself enough to draw boundaries to protect his service so he could write the books he wrote. I'm glad he faithfully served the position God gave him. And I'm glad for how God continues to multiply Luke's service even after Luke has been gone from this world for nearly two thousand years.

Become you, and serve. It's yes to both. Then serve as you. Be faithful to God who both calls you who you are and calls you to serve. Walk with him through the times when it feels these callings contradict each other and let him help you wrestle through it. It's all a good thing and part of the process.

And then rejoice, because you are becoming who you were born to be *and* you are impacting the world in a powerful way.

Chapter 7

THE TREE OF DEATH

Christians make long lists of rules they think they must live by, but this isn't the kind of life God intended for us. Looking through history, we discover that rules were never really very important to God and we learn when and why he made rules at all. Ultimately, we discover that rules lead to independence from God and death, a hopeless life in which we need God to save us not just from death, but from the rules that brought it in the first place.

Many Christians think life is all about rules. What's more, I think most Christians truly think God wants us to live in this rule-conscious way. That's certainly what I believed for a long time, until one conversation with God destroyed everything I had previously understood about what he desired from my life.

God introduced me to this mind-bending truth while on a hunting trip a number of years ago. Early in the morning at the hotel, I was getting my things out of the way for the other hunters in my party. As the youngest in the group, my bedroom was essentially the hallway floor. Nothing seemed out of the ordinary this day, other than that I was cleaning my room at 4:30 in the morning, but out of the blue God asked me a question. He asked, "How could Adam and Eve have sinned while they lived in the garden?"

I knew it must be a setup. God only asks questions to teach us something, not because he needs us to tell him the answer. I thought for a while and cautiously guessed, "Only if they ate from the tree of the knowledge of good and evil?"

There was a lot more to this, and God wasn't done. My mind began to stir with the ramifications of this answer. It was as though God was asking me a follow-up question, "Just that one way? What about all the other rules I gave people later on? What if they broke one of those?"

Now I was trapped. The obvious answer went against anything I'd ever learned about how much God cared about us following his laws, everything I knew about how to define sin, but I couldn't come up with any other answer except the obvious one. And, of course, the obvious answer is that Adam and Eve could have broken any of God's other laws without being removed from the garden because he had never told them not to do those things.

That leaves us with a lot of questions. I mean, we think of breaking God's rules as sin, and we teach that Adam led humankind into the fall by sinning. Hypothetically, let's say Adam and Eve never ate from the forbidden tree. Let's say their children were born in the garden, and after they grew up one stole something from the other. Would that have led humankind into sin? Would it have led to the fall? Would it have even been considered sin, since God had never forbidden it? What word could you use to describe that act if you can't describe it as sin? Or if it is still sin, how does it not have power in the same way Adam's disobedience did, leading all humankind into sin and death?

It doesn't take long in going down that path before you start to question everything you thought you knew about sin, God's relationship to humankind, our relationship to him, and what he desires of us. But we need to answer these questions, because it all starts with that obvious first answer God led me to that day—that there truly was only one way for Adam and Eve to sin in a way that led to death, and it had nothing to do with the Ten Commandments or any of the other rules we think we need to follow today. Ultimately, here were the heavyweight questions: First, if Adam and Eve didn't need to follow God's other rules like the Ten Commandments, why not? Second, what does that mean for us today?

THE TESTIMONY OF HISTORY

There was no doubt in my mind that I had to answer these questions. I was possessed of a curiosity mixed with fearful wonder. Since God posed the question to me regarding a particular time in history—Adam and Eve in the garden—I decided to look through biblical history to see what that would tell me. I was surprised that it told me a lot.

I tracked one question through the timeline of history. I wanted to discover what people at various points of history understood about what God required of them. The garden is obviously the very beginning of history, and just to be thorough, we'll start there. From what God communicated to Adam and Eve, here is the exhaustive list of everything they could have known God wanted from their lives: Be fruitful and multiply. Rule the earth and subdue it. Cultivate and keep the garden. Eat from any tree except from the tree of the knowledge of good and evil.

That's it. Those four things comprised all the requirements God placed on Adam and Eve. Those were the boundaries for their behavior. I mean, those were the *only* boundaries. Imagine what your life would be like if you thought those four things were all God wanted of you. What if you had absolutely no awareness of any sort that there could possibly be more expected of you than that? How much freedom would you have to do absolutely anything you wanted to do?

Let me clarify this a bit by modernizing the language to what it would mean for us today. Have a family (remember, in God's perfect garden there wouldn't be infertility, miscarriages, or any other difficulties with this; plus, neither you nor your spouse would have sin in your lives, so marriage would be much easier). Take what God's given you and grow it. Maintain what you grow or build. Don't eat from the tree that will teach you to live from rules instead of God's example.

If that were your life, you would have the freedom you needed to become what you were created to be. You would have the freedom to dream, to step out and try things, to fail and get back up again, and keep going toward those dreams because nothing told you what not to do. You would know your job is only to multiply and take dominion, to go for it, to take risks and try new things and see what will happen. And you'd have no list of shoulds to make you ashamed of when you failed, so no cords of condemnation could get ahold on you to keep you from your dreams.

That's the life Adam and Eve had until the day they ate from the tree of the knowledge of good and evil. Isn't it interesting, though, that when God forced Adam and Eve to leave the garden, he didn't give them any more rules. They didn't have anything more to go on except what they already had to help them understand what God desired or required of them. Go ahead and read Genesis 3, but you won't find any extra rules there anywhere.

We can move on through history to Genesis 4 and 5, which record the genealogy of the first generations of humankind from Adam to Noah. Noteworthy here is how long people lived. It was common for the men listed to have lived eight or nine hundred years (no women are listed), so while it may not have been many generations, it was 1,656 years from Adam's creation to the flood. Noah was building the ark during the last hundred years of that period of time.

We can surmise that there was some understanding of what God required of people for two reasons. First, Cain and Abel made sacrifices, so it seems they had some understanding of a system of worship. Second, humankind had some semblance of an understanding of righteousness, or there wouldn't have been a contrast between Noah and everyone else. What we don't have is any record that there was any sort of system of rules that governed peoples' relationship with God. We have no record of a written or oral tradition to lead the people in this beyond the basic codes of ethics and morality that have always been common to all societies worldwide, accompanied by some tradition of how to worship whichever deity you chose.

If you study any level of anthropology (the study of human behavior and culture), you'll find pretty quickly that cultures all over the world throughout all time have always had a fairly consistent standard of right and wrong. Greek and Roman philosophers had elaborate beliefs on ethics and morality, and even most tribal cultures throughout the world have pretty much the same morality. Actually, it's pretty amazing how universal the human-relationships side of the Ten Commandments really is in cultural codes throughout the diverse human civilizations. Almost everyone prohibits or frowns upon murder, theft, adultery, and the like. It's not like you need the Bible to give people these kinds of basic laws of morality.

Yes, you also find that, universally, all over the world, people violate those basic laws, but they do still exist throughout all cultures—pagan, Christian, tribal, and sophisticated. This common morality actually makes sense, because it comes from what happened in the garden. Adam ate from the tree of the knowledge of good and evil, which put into each one of his descendants the innate sense of right and wrong. This is a hugely significant point, and one that we'll return to later in the timeline.

WALKING WITH GOD

While we don't have record of any written or oral tradition of rules God had given people to live by, we do have an interesting note said about two different people. The same thing is said about Enoch and Noah—they walked with God.

Genesis 5:22–24 is where you can find it saying this about Enoch. Incredibly, he walked so closely with God that one day God simply took him off the earth: "Enoch walked with God; and he was not, for God took him" (v. 24). Genesis 6:9 talks about Noah: "Noah was a righteous man, blameless in his time; Noah walked with God."

The significance of these two verses is that these men *walked with God*. Listen, they walked with God before any of the sacrificial systems of the law were set up, before Jesus restored us to God, and before any systematic form of worship was established. They had no Day of Atonement, no ark of the covenant, no mercy seat, and no high priest. No one stood before God on their behalf, and, as far as we know, no sacrifice had atoned for their sins even in a prophetic and symbolic sense, foreshadowing Jesus' ultimate sacrifice. They simply walked with God!

But who told them they were allowed to do that? Before I started searching this out, I had thought sin was supposed to have separated us from God so that we couldn't do that anymore. Yet here they were, two men who were considered righteous, of whom it was said they walked with God.

We find more clarity about what this looks like when we get to the other side of the flood. Moving on to Genesis 10 and 11, we can read the generations from Shem (Noah's son) to Abraham. This takes us to 367 years after the flood, and Abram (not yet Abraham) is seventy-five years old and just leaving Haran.

If you walk through Abram's life, he also had no religious code, orally given or written, that we have any record of. God simply spoke to him, saying, "Leave the land of your fathers and I will show you a land I will give you," and Abram obeyed. Yes, we do see him making sacrifices along the way and raising some altars, but later when God gave laws to Israel, he gave specific rules about how they should and should not do even those simple things. Abraham clearly had no rules about this, no laws about how to make altars or what to sacrifice on them. It was purely a form of worship, or in other words, a form of declaring who he worshiped—that the Lord was his God.

What we do have from Abraham's life is something I already alluded to, that God spoke to him and Abraham obeyed. God said go and he went. God gave him a promise and he believed. In other words, Abraham walked with God. It is this belief, recorded in Genesis 15:6, that changes history. Scripture here declares, "Then he believed in the Lord; and he reckoned it to him as righteousness." Abraham's righteousness

THE TREE OF DEATH

had nothing to do with the following of any law. In fact, it had nothing to do with anything that any other human could have done, because it had to do with a specific promise to a specific person at a specific time. But Abraham believed God, so God called him righteous.

How incredible is it that Abraham didn't do anything for that declaration? He didn't work hard to follow a list of rules and dos and don'ts. He had no "Thou shalt" or "Thou shalt not" chasing him down to determine his course of action. He simply had the voice of God leading him each step of the way.

I really want you to try to get into his mindset and think about what Abraham would have understood about God at this point in history. Moses wouldn't even be born for several hundred more years. Mount Sinai was nearly half a millennium away from happening. Abraham was as removed from those eventual historical events as we are from Christopher Columbus. It would be like us trying to understand what life might be like in year AD 2600. He had no grid for it, and, like us, probably gave it no thought.

You can look for yourself if you like. What rules did he have about how he lived? Go ahead and search his whole story, but you won't find rules of any kind. You will only find that God gave him Abraham-specific instructions that you and I couldn't follow even if we were desperate to try. That's what it looked like for these men to walk with God. Walking with God was the only way for them to know how to live, because they had no rules to tell them how to live apart from him.

This pattern continues through the generations of Abraham through Joseph and his brothers. And just to save time and space, we'll skip through quite a bit of their history to arrive at the very first Passover. Just a few weeks later, you would find the nation of Israel gathered around Mount Sinai where God began giving them the law. It is now 1446 BC.

Let me tell you a little about this date. It is 645 years after Abram left Haran, 1,012 years after the flood, and 2,668 years after creation. Let's do some simple math. If you take that 2,668 years, add the 1,446 years until Jesus' birth, and then add the 2,016 years since then at the time of my writing this, you get a total number of 6,130 years of human history. So those first 2,668 years before God gave the law on Mount Sinai amount to 44 percent of human history.

Cut away the numbers to get to the point: almost half of human history took place before God gave the law. Even though it only takes roughly fifty chapters of the Bible (the book of Genesis) to tell that much of our collective story, it's still a crucial thing for us to understand. It's important because we get to see how humankind related to God for all those years without any rules or laws.

They walked with him, by faith. That's all. Their relationship with God wasn't defined by rules or laws, but instead by the fact that he's alive, he spoke to them, and they followed him.

And when you take just the 1,479 years during which the law was God's primary way of interacting with humankind (adding on 33 years for Jesus' life), you find it was only 24 percent of our history, and it lessens every year.

WHAT DOES THIS MEAN?

If you grew up in church, you know the rules. You know what happens when people break the rules too. Christianity calls for boycotts of unrighteous people, nations, industries, or companies. Pastors ask unrepentant sinners to stop darkening their doors, and sometimes prevent them from entering a first time. Leaders declare that God will judge cities (New Orleans), states (California), or countries (the United States) that we perceived to be the greatest violators of God's laws. We have built a culture as pertains to sin that makes us all put on our best face for an hour or two every Sunday, pretending we have no sin issues in our lives, before we retreat home again where all too often we turn to addictions, anger, abuse, selfish living, and taking to Facebook to tell the rest of the world how wicked it is.

This is our culture of rules, where rules rule the day, and we make it this way because we think these rules are super important to God. So here are my questions: If rules are that important to God, why did he wait until halfway through human history before he told us his rules? Why would he do that to all the people who lived before then? Also, if God's rules are that important to him, then why did he never mention them to the people who walked with him? Why did he instead talk to these people about how he promised to bless them, save them, and make them great? And if he waited so long to give his rules, why did God finally choose to give them when he did?

Because it wasn't on accident. He didn't give his rules at that specific point in history as a way of throwing up his hands, resigning himself to the fact that those stupid humans would just never understand what he expected of them otherwise. He had a specific, strategic plan and purpose for doing it how he did it when he did it. It didn't happen without incredible planning and forethought.

I believe it all ties back to the garden and the choice made by Adam and Eve to eat from the tree of the knowledge of good and evil. See, there were two trees in the garden—the tree of life and the tree of the knowledge of good and evil. I believe that each of these trees represents a system under which humankind could have chosen to live. One is obviously a system where life thrives. The other is a system defined by knowing good and evil, right and wrong.

Ever since Adam ate from that tree, human existence has been defined by the lists of shoulds—and where there are shoulds, there is shame. Over the course of time, God continued to relate to men and women the way he did in the beginning, just simply by speaking to the ones who would walk with him. However, when he chose a nation for himself, that required a different form of leadership.

Make no mistake about God's intentions, however. When he gave the law, he intended to have an intimate relationship with every individual, beginning with every Israeli individual. God declared his intention for them, saying, "And you shall be to me a kingdom of priests and a holy nation" (Exodus 19:6). He desired that all of Israel would stand as priests before him to minister in his presence and hear his voice, that all of them—every man, woman, and child—would have that intimate encounter with him. And, of course, all those priests weren't supposed to be priests mediating for one another. God's purpose was to make Israel his priestly nation to mediate for him and all the other nations in order to reconcile the entire world to himself.

But when God spoke to the people, they were terrified and said, "Moses, you go talk to God for us, because if he speaks to us again, we will all die" (my paraphrase of Exodus 20:1–22). More than that, the tribe of Levi was the only one to return to the Lord after the rebellion in worshiping the golden calf, and that is why the other eleven tribes were rejected from being priests to God. God's intent was for everyone to draw near, but they removed themselves far from him.

Israel repeated this pattern again when they asked for a king, as God declared to Samuel, "Obey the voice of the people in all that they say to you, for they have not rejected you, but they have rejected me from being king over them" (1 Samuel 8:7). Again God invited them to intimacy and relationship, but again they ran away from him and insisted on a human to stand in God's place instead.

In all of this, we can still see God's heart! His heart is to have intimacy with us, to draw near to us and walk with us. That has always been his invitation, even when he invited an entire nation to do that as one person. The law he gave them was simply a contract—a covenant—that defined his agreement with them as his nation. He promised them that if they followed his rules, they would be blessed. They would have dominion over the land he promised to give them. Their crops and harvests would be blessed, as well as their herds and flocks. Their own wombs and offspring would be blessed and would not miscarry. They would be blessed in many, many ways, if only they would follow the rules.

WHY RULES?

Someone could wonder why God gave his rules in the first place. I mean, it's great that he wants relationship with humankind and that the law served as his invitation for all people to become intimate with him again, but that's not what happened. The rules only produced shame, and God certainly knew they would, so why did he give them?

The short answer is that God gave the laws he did to honor his promise to Adam and then Adam's choice. Let me explain.

In the beginning, as I've said repeatedly, God made us to be like him. But the second part of his declaration over us was, "And let them have dominion" (Genesis 1:26). The dominion God endowed on Adam and Eve gave them authority over all the earth and over absolutely every creature on the earth, whether on land, in the water, or in the air. He put us in charge of this planet.

Then he gave us freedom of choice. It was the only way our dominion could truly be ours and not his, which was the only way for us to learn to become like him. This couldn't be some sort of safe test zone where mistakes didn't matter. No, this was live-fire, not-a-drill stuff. Not only was our free will the only way our love for him could be meaningful, but our free will was also the only way for us to become like him, because he has free will.

So when Adam used his free will to choose disobedience, it had consequences far beyond himself. One consequence was that when he chose to eat from the tree of the knowledge of good and evil, it meant he determined the way all his descendants would interact with life and the world around them. Now things like righteousness and sin, good and evil, and right and wrong could be known and measured by us apart from any other influence in our life.

Before Adam ate from that tree, he and Eve (and all their descendants) were dependent upon God to know how to live. Our only choice was to humbly walk with God, just like Enoch, Noah, and Abraham. But once Adam ate that fruit, we now had an option to try to do life on our own. We didn't have to walk with God to try to live a good life; we could live independent from him because we had our own sense of right and wrong.

It's actually this independence that leads to death, because we can't achieve God-likeness on our own efforts. We can only do it by walking with him. No rules can produce God-likeness and fulfill the reason God made us. So if we live by rules, by independence, by knowing right from wrong, we will sin and fall short of what God intended for us. In falling short, we walk down the path to death because we are walking alone and not in partnership with and dependence on God. God is life, so independence from him will always lead to death.

God knew this, of course, but he also knew he gave Adam the authority to make choices that matter, and he wasn't going back on it. In God's free will, he chose to honor Adam's choice while still providing a way for people to have relationship with him.

That way is the law. It defines good and evil, satisfying the method Adam chose for humankind to relate to God and the world around them. It also provided ways for them to be forgiven—to ditch the shame that plagued them and start brand-new. God mercifully included the yearly Day of Atonement, during which all the sins of the people would be placed on one solitary goat that was then sent to wander in the wilderness alone. God also mercifully provided Sabbath years every seven years and the ultimate Year of Jubilee every fifty years, where all debt was canceled, all property returned to its original owners, and all slaves set free. God declared that the name of his throne was the mercy seat, and he invited people into the blessings of life through faith in him and walking in his ways.

And what were the laws, really? Sure, some had to do with health and safety, like laws of diseases and diet, but most of the laws taught the people how to be like him. I mean, have you ever wondered why God gave the laws he did? It's not like he was just sitting in heaven one day and arbitrarily chose the things he said were right and wrong.

No, he chose rules that would lead people into their original created identity—being like him! He told them, "Do not murder," because he is the author of life! He told them, "Do not steal," because he is generous! He told them, "Do not commit adultery," because he is faithful! He told them, "Do not covet," because he is our provider! If we walk with him and become like him, then we do not need these rules. After all, God does not need the rules; he only needs to be himself.

THE TREE OF DEATH

WHAT RULES CAN AND CAN'T DO

But now we begin to understand both the power and the powerlessness of the rules God gave Israel. While every rule was an invitation to wonder, *What does this rule teach me about God's nature, and how I can be like him?* it seems no one asked that question. They took the rules at face value, which is the absolutely natural thing to do, and so the rules only served to separate them from God further, tying them to a religious system of moral conduct rooted in the hopeless effort of human strength trying to become like the infinite God.

Of course, God knew it would lead to one desperate conclusion—that we can't be like God in our own effort. We need a savior, and not just any savior. We need God to save us not just from the rules but also from the choice Adam made for us six thousand years ago that still haunts us today.

You might wonder what I have against rules. Am I some antiestablishment anarchist? Hardly. I grew up in good rules-oriented churches that preached the gospel of salvation, taught against sin, and regularly offered the chance for people to repent. My Southern Baptist roots helped me memorize a ton of Scripture, especially during those weeks when we had revival services every evening all week long with nightly altar calls for repentance and salvation.

Then, sometime after I moved to Minnesota, I gave myself fully to the rules, trying to do everything I could to follow every last one of them. I went to every Bible study. I participated enthusiastically in multiple versions of accountability groups, confessing my sins weekly to my peers. I read my Bible and prayed every day, filling pages of my journals with the cry of my heart that God would help me stop breaking his rules. I even reprimanded my unsaved teammates if they cussed around me and gritted my teeth through anytime I had to listen to secular music.

Rules were how I lived for Jesus. That was all I knew. I thought godliness meant the same thing as morality, instead of what it literally means: God-like-ness. I was taught that sin is what separates us from God, and that sin is breaking God's laws. I was taught clearly and then shown in the way all the believers around me lived that Jesus' death reserved a spot for us in heaven but didn't fully deliver us from sin on earth. My own experience only caused me to agree all the more fully with this teaching.

The whole sum of it led me to a life completely obsessed with the rules, the fear of breaking them, and the shame of having broken them. I bent myself entirely toward verses like Romans 12:1, "I appeal to you therefore, brothers, by the mercies of God, to present your bodies as a living sacrifice"; Philippians 1:21, "For to me to live is Christ, and to die is gain"; Galatians 2:19–20, "I have been crucified with Christ. It is no longer I who live, but Christ who lives in me"; and Matthew 16:24, "If anyone would come after me, let him deny himself and take up his cross and follow me."

I surrounded myself with symbols of Christian extremism, living for the voices that called me to die every day for Jesus. I understood those passages about being a living sacrifice—to live as Christ, to be crucified with Christ, and to take up my cross—to mean needed to white-knuckle my way into righteous living through my own efforts. I thought that if I just died more to myself, then I would somehow find the ability to stop sinning, to stop lusting, to stop being selfish, to stop being afraid, and to stop being angry.

Guess what? None of it worked. I tried with all my might for ten years and met little improvement in how I lived. If you've tried the same methods, you've most likely met with the same results. Of course, everyone would meet with those results, because rules never had the power to transform even one single life. Rules only had the power to identify the sin we already had as what it is and to show us how desperately we need a savior, not just from the sin but from the rules that can actually keep us trapped in sin.

God let me bury myself in a form of Christianity that had no power to transform my life. He led me through that time of fully embracing the religious process of morality so I could experience for myself how completely powerless it is.

THE TREE OF DEATH

But then he saved me from it, and in that salvation I also found the freedom and transformation I had longed for so desperately. God taught me the way Jesus lived his life perfectly, how it had nothing to do with memorizing rules, and he showed me that because of Jesus, we can live just like he did. And in living as Jesus did, we can find the life we were born to live.

Chapter 8

THE TREE OF LIFE

God never intended Christians to live by rules, but instead for us to live by the Holy Spirit until we become like him. In this life, God's identity is the standard for our living, wisdom teaches us how to live, and the process of becoming like God starts by simply becoming his child.

Reading so much about rules, failure, shame, and condemnation probably makes you want to do the same thing it makes me want to do: run and hide. This has almost always been the human response to these things. Thankfully, I'll take you to the complete opposite place in this chapter. The first step we'll take together is to challenge one of the core beliefs we've had that makes us think we're separated from God.

I can still remember clearly what it was like the first time I went on a mission trip. The team I was part of had about a dozen meetings ahead of time to cover all sorts of things that would help us be ready for what we'd signed up to do. One of the most important of these meetings trained us in a few simple evangelism tools. The first one is well-known, so you may have heard of it. It's called the Bridge Illustration. I'll walk you through it.

First, imagine a stick-figure person standing at the edge of a cliff. You can tell they are looking far over the edge to where they can see another cliff rising on the other side of a chasm. This, according to my training, describes the state of every man, woman, and child when they are born. They are on one side of the chasm, but God is on the other side. In between God and man is this great divide, an insurmountable distance hopelessly keeping us from God and heaven. We learned that this great divide is called sin. Sin is what separates us from God.

This is where the strength of this illustration comes, as you can easily show how no one is able to create a way across this chasm through their own good works. They cannot cross it by their own strength or effort. The only possible solution could not come from humankind but instead had to come from God. The illustration is so simple that you could have been drawing it on a napkin while having coffee with an unsaved friend. At this point you simply draw a cross from one cliff to the other, bridging the gap between the two and showing how Jesus' work on the cross is the only thing that can break the separation between us and God.

Honestly, I love this tool. I think it's great, and I personally know several people who use this to regularly lead people to a relationship with Jesus. However, like so many other traditional tools, beliefs, and sayings that I've mentioned so far, I think this is another good start that we need to examine again to see if it's the whole truth. Because, as I look at Scripture, I honestly can't find anywhere that teaches that sin separates us from God.

THE MYSTERY OF SEPARATION

Through tools like the one above, I had always believed that sin separates us from God and that if any sinner somehow found their way into God's holy presence they would die. This taught me a view of God that saw him not just as holy and righteous but also as vengeful, wrathful, stiff, and uncaring. He was a Father quick to discipline with the harshest of means for the simple violation of someone coming to be with him. In the rule-driven, performance-oriented way of thinking I knew at the time, we called this the fear of God that produces wisdom, a healthy reverence for a holy God. It was just one piece of my God-good/humankind-bad belief system.

Then a day came when, all of a sudden, I realized that I couldn't think of a single example of anyone in Scripture who actually died from entering God's presence, and that, instead, I could think of many people who entered God's presence and lived. This led me to investigate the timeline of history again, similar to how I did before, to see how much God really cared about rules.

What I found begins with Adam and Eve. Immediately after they sinned, we read this:

> Then the eyes of both were opened, and they knew that they were naked. And they sewed fig leaves together and made themselves loincloths. And they heard the sound of the Lord God walking in the garden in the cool of the day, *and the man and his wife hid themselves from the presence of the Lord God* among the trees of the garden. But the Lord God called to the man and said to him, "Where are you?" And he said, "I heard the sound of you in the garden, and I was afraid, because I was naked, and I hid myself."—Genesis 3:7–10

The situation here is clear. Adam and Eve had fallen into sin. They were no longer God's perfect creation, but had now become the fallen creation that is supposed to be unwelcome in God's presence. Yet here it isn't Adam or Eve who pursue God in any way; instead it is God who draws near to them. Certainly he knew what had happened. He knew it would happen before he ever made them, so he was not ignorant, surprised, or caught off-guard. Like his question, "Where are you?" he didn't really need Adam to answer in order to know where he was and what had happened.

No, it wasn't God who removed himself from their sinful presence. It was Adam and Eve who ran from God's presence because of their shame.

You can look at God's curse that followed the verses above, where he first curses Satan, then Eve, then Adam, and nowhere in those verses does he curse humankind's relationship with him. His curse is between us and our human relationships and between us and our relationship with the land. The only reference to our relationship with him comes in his promise that one day the seed of woman would crush Satan's head, a prophecy about how Jesus would save us.

You can also look at how Adam and Eve were cast out of the garden, but it was to remove them from the tree of life so that they wouldn't live eternally in sin, not so that they would be removed from God's presence. Nowhere in this story does it say anything about God removing himself from them, only about them hiding from him.

A HISTORY OF ENCOUNTER

As the story of humankind goes on, you see that Enoch and Noah walked with God, as I talked about in the last chapter. Neither of them died because of their encounters. As well, the life of Abraham gives us completely unambiguous accounts of how he physically encountered God on at least two separate occasions.

First, he met Melchizedek in Genesis 14 after he rescued Lot. Melchizedek is called a priest to the Most High God, but we know that he is actually a form of incarnate Jesus before Jesus was actually born. He was God in the flesh, and Abraham didn't die (neither did any of the other hundreds of men with him during that encounter).

Another time during Abraham's life, the Lord came physically with two angels to Abraham's tent and ate a meal with him, promising that one year from that time he would have a son with Sarah. This is when Sarah laughed, which led them to name their son Isaac, which means laughter (this story is found in Genesis 18).

Jacob wrestles with God all night long in another physical encounter. Once he realized who he wrestled with, Jacob named the place Peniel, which means "face of God." He did this because he realized he had seen

God's face yet didn't die (Genesis 32).

Moses' life is filled with encounters with God that didn't kill him. He had the burning bush in Exodus 3 and 4 and several encounters at Mount Sinai in Exodus 19 to 40. Early in their time at Mount Sinai, before Moses went up to receive the Ten Commandments from the Lord, God commanded Moses to bring Aaron and two of his sons, Nadab and Abihu, and the seventy elders of Israel part way up the mountain with him. Here is what we read about that:

> Then Moses and Aaron, Nadab, and Abihu, and seventy of the elders of Israel went up, and they saw the God of Israel. There was under his feet as it were a pavement of sapphire stone, like the very heaven for clearness. And he did not lay his hand on the chief men of the people of Israel; they beheld God, and ate and drank.—Exodus 24:9–11

Here we have seventy-four people who all beheld God with their physical eyes, and this time it's not just a physical, humanlike manifestation of him. This is the full-on, true, spiritual vision of God that they saw with their own eyes, and none of them died. Instead, they had a meal together in God's presence.

Moses is noted for having the tent of meeting, where he regularly went to meet with God. This is where he would go when the people brought issues to him that he needed God's help to resolve. The entire nation of Israel would stand by their tent and watch as God's presence descended upon this tent to speak with Moses face-to-face. Oh, and Joshua always went with him, staying behind even after Moses would leave (Exodus 33:7–11).

We can move on to Judges, where Gideon met the angel of the Lord and said, "Alas, O Lord God! For now I have seen the angel of the Lord face to face." Instead of killing him, God makes peace with him and Gideon names God "The Lord is Peace" (Judges 6:22–24). This encounter didn't kill him, but it did launch Gideon into a great purpose and destiny.

Samson's mother meets the angel of the Lord twice and his father meets him once, after which his father says, just like Gideon, "Oh no! We're going to die!" Samson's mother wisely replies, "If God meant to kill us, he wouldn't have made these great promises to us." Again, just like Gideon, the encounter didn't kill them but instead launched them into greatness.

King David made the presence of God his highest priority. As soon as he was king over all Israel, he moved the ark of the covenant into Jerusalem, pitching a huge tent for it in his backyard and paying thousands of musicians to worship in the presence of God around the clock every day of the year. David himself had enough Gentile blood in him because of his Moabite great-grandmother, Ruth, that he shouldn't have even been allowed to assemble with Israel before the tabernacle, according to Moses' laws (Deuteronomy 23:3), yet he was the one leading the procession in God's presence and regularly went into the tent to worship God. During this thirty-three-year period of Israel's history, thousands of people went into God's presence and none of them died. Instead, this is looked upon as the golden age of Israel's history.

Elijah survived God's presence on Mount Sinai in 1 Kings 19. Isaiah also survived God's presence in Isaiah 6 when the voices of the cherubim shook the foundations of the temple, and more than surviving, this encounter launched the ministry of the prophet who spoke more about Jesus than any other prophet. Ezekiel also survived an encounter with God so profound that it takes up the entire first three chapters of the book that bears his name. Instead of dying, this was the beginning of his prophetic ministry.

Let me not fail to mention every single high priest ever, for well over a thousand years. And of course, we can't forget the first thirty-three years of Jesus' life before he paid for our sins, living with countless people, and the only one who died was him.

All of these men and women encountered God—physically, face-to-face, spiritually in open heavens, and otherwise—and all of them lived. Many of them thought they were going to die, but none of them did.

This is a powerful truth! It means that all this time God has not been holding himself back from humankind, but instead we have been hiding from him. All these thousands of people found encounters with God even during the Old Testament before Jesus' sacrifice tore the veil of the Holy of Holies. How much more is the invitation open to every one of us to come and be with him?

We just need to stop hiding. It's that shame thing again. It makes us want to hide, but I'll tell you what, we won't ever find the cure for our shame hiding by ourselves or commiserating with other people who have the same shame. We're only going to overcome our shame and the sin that caused it by vulnerably coming to our good Father like children who've been playing in the mud when they shouldn't have and letting him toss us in the bath of his love to clean us off and remind us who we are—his chosen sons and daughters made to be just like him.

GOD STILL HAS A STANDARD

Understanding that God never removed us from himself, but that we removed ourselves from his presence is a huge step toward leaving behind the Tree of Death that taught us to live by rules, laws, and regulations. The whole point of all those rules is to try to act like God in our own strength in the hope that it will be enough for him to approve us for fellowship again. It's all about performing for acceptance, but he never stopped accepting us.

Yes, sin always brings death and eventually it does lead to eternal separation from God in the lake of fire. Yes, because of that, Jesus had to die as the propitiation for our sins, as I wrote in an earlier chapter. But the idea that people on earth are separated from God because of their sin in a way that means they cannot enter his presence just isn't biblical.

Every time I talk to Christians about living a life independent from the rules we have all thought we need to live by, their very first concern is the question of how we are to live our lives. We all understand that God does have a standard he expects us to live by. We can see how the rules only hurt us, and we can even see how we should then cut them out of our lives. What is not as easy to see is what we should replace them with.

Well, when I began writing about the two trees, I made the statement that I believe both trees were a system under which humankind could have lived. Adam chose the system of rules, of independence from God. Jesus is the one who reveals to us how to live in the second system, the system of the tree of life.

FULFILLING THE LAW

One of the first things Jesus did after starting his public ministry was preach the Sermon on the Mount. During one early section of that sermon, he clarified the purpose of his ministry:

> "Do not think that I have come to abolish the Law or the Prophets; I have not come to abolish them but to fulfill them. For truly, I say to you, until heaven and earth pass away, not an iota, not a dot, will pass from the Law until all is accomplished. Therefore whoever relaxes one of the least of these commandments and teaches others to do the same will be called least in the kingdom of heaven, but whoever does them and teaches them will be called great in the kingdom of heaven. For I tell you, unless your righteousness exceeds that of the scribes and Pharisees, you will never enter the kingdom of heaven."—Matthew 5:17–20

Jesus made clear that the testimony of the law and prophets aren't going anywhere until heaven and earth pass away. That makes sense, because until that time Adam's choice of the knowledge of good and evil is still at work within all his children. But Jesus also said he came to fulfill the law and prophets, which means something has significantly changed for those of us who put our faith in him. His conclusion to this section helps us understand something about what this fulfillment looks like and what it means to us.

He says that our righteousness has to exceed that of the scribes and Pharisees, but how are we supposed to do that? When Paul talked about being a Pharisee, he said he was blameless under the law (Philippians 3:6). That's what the Pharisee life was all about, so how are we supposed to do better than that?

I've been told several times that the following parts of Jesus' sermon explain this as he makes statements like "You have heard it said, 'Do not commit adultery.' But I say to you that everyone who looks at a woman with lustful intent has committed adultery in his heart" (Matthew 5:27–28) and "You have heard it said, 'Do not murder.' But I say to you that everyone who is angry with his brother will be liable to judgment" (Matthew 5:21–22). I was taught, "Look, Jesus made the law even harder! We have a stricter law now than in the Old Testament." I think this misses Jesus' point.

After Jesus says our righteousness must exceed that of the scribes and Pharisees, he embarks on a journey through sixteen different topics. Most of them include some sort of comparison between what the people had been taught and what Jesus now taught them, or a comparison between what they had seen in the Pharisees and what he now taught them. Here are a few examples:

"You have heard that it was said to those of old, 'You shall not murder; and whoever murders will be liable to judgment.' But I say to you that everyone who is angry with his brother will be liable to judgment."—Matthew 5:21–22

"You have heard that it was said, 'You shall not commit adultery.' But I say to you that everyone who looks at a woman with lustful intent has already committed adultery with her *in his heart*." —Matthew 5:27–28

"Beware of practicing your righteousness *before other people in order to be seen by them*, for then you will have no reward from your Father who is in heaven. Thus, when you give to the needy, sound no trumpet before you, as the hypocrites do in the synagogues and in the streets, that they may be praised by others."—Matthew 6:1–2

"And when you pray, you must not be like the hypocrites. For they love to stand and pray in the synagogues and at the street corners, *that they may be seen by others*. … But when you pray, go into your room and shut the door and *pray to your Father who is in secret*."—Matthew 6:5–6

"And when you fast, do not look gloomy like the hypocrites, for they disfigure their faces *that their fasting may be seen by others*. … But when you fast, anoint your head and wash your face, that *your fasting may not be seen by others but by your Father who is in secret*."—Matthew 6:16–18

"Beware of false prophets, who come to you in sheep's clothing, but *inwardly are ravenous wolves*. You will recognize them by their fruits."—Matthew 7:15–16

The consistent theme throughout Jesus' teachings in the Sermon on the Mount is the difference between a life lived righteously on the outside for the sake of public recognition and a life of inward righteousness that lives unto God. The main point here is outward performance versus inward righteousness.

Jesus was showing us that the way we exceed the righteousness of the scribes and Pharisees is to cultivate a righteousness of the heart. Their righteousness was only skin deep, which is why Jesus later called them whitewashed tombs and cups washed only on the outside. They outwardly put on a great show for all to see, but their insides were full of death. Jesus called them hypocrites, which didn't mean quite the same then as it does now. In Jesus' day, *hypocrite* was the Greek word for actors: someone pretending to be something they really aren't. That's what the scribes and Pharisees were doing—acting like righteous people when that wasn't genuinely who they were.

Their biggest problem, though, wasn't that they were acting; it was that they thought they were authentic. They thought their act had the power to make them righteous because they thought righteousness was only about performing rules and rituals, forgetting completely about their hearts.

THE WISDOM OF GOD'S WORDS

If Jesus had stopped there, we would be lost. We wouldn't know how to keep this from simply being another list of shoulds that would bring shame because of our inevitable failure to change our own hearts by working hard to make it happen. Thankfully, he didn't stop there. These are the concluding words to his sermon:

> "Everyone then who *hears these words of mine and does them will be like a wise man* who built his house on the rock. And the rain fell, and the floods came, and the winds blew and beat on that house, but it did not fall, because it had been founded on the rock. And everyone who *hears these words of mine and does not do them will be like a foolish man* who built his house on the sand. And the rain fell, and the floods came, and the winds blew and beat against that house, and it fell, and great was the fall of it."
> —Matthew 7:24–27

There are two important keys in the contrast Jesus makes for us here. The first is that the distinction is between two people who heard Jesus' words; one does them and one does not. Hearing Jesus' words is about much more than reading this sermon he preached and then walking away from him to try to do it on our own. That's a good try at obeying what he says here, but I believe he intends the hearing and doing to be part of our ongoing relationship with him. Otherwise it simply reverts back to the laws that no one had the power to follow anyway and the righteousness that's only skin-deep.

The second key we see here is that Jesus says those who obey his words are wise and those who do not are foolish. This is an interesting and important departure from using the words *righteous* and *unrighteous* or the words *obedient* and *disobedient*. Jesus is telling us that the pathway to being able to live a righteous and godly life is wisdom, not rules, and that we will only discover wisdom by walking in a relationship with him where we continually abide in his words.

We can know for certain this is what Jesus meant, because this is exactly how Jesus himself lived his perfectly righteous life. I've looked many times through Jesus' life, and while he obviously knew the Scriptures, he also never once says anything about working to live by this rule or that. In fact, the "experts" when it came to the rules called him out over and over again for things he did that they thought broke God's rules.

While Jesus never once cited the laws that guided his day-by-day and moment-by-moment decisions and actions, he did clearly tell us what led him to do what he did. He said he only did what he saw his Father doing and said what he heard his Father saying (John 5:19; 12:49). In other words, he did exactly what he told us we should do. He listened to his Father's words and did them and taught us to listen to his words and do them. This was how Jesus lived his life, not by rules but by wisdom.

If there were any other doubt that this truly is how Jesus lived his life, a prophecy from Isaiah 11 makes it perfectly clear:

> There shall come forth a shoot from the stump of Jesse, and a branch from his roots shall bear fruit. *And the Spirit of the Lord shall rest upon him, the Spirit of wisdom* and understanding, the Spirit of counsel and might, the Spirit of knowledge and the fear

of the LORD. And his delight shall be in the fear of the LORD. He shall not judge by what his eyes see, or decide disputes by what his ears hear, but *with righteousness he shall judge the poor*, and decide with equity for the meek of the earth; and he shall strike the earth with the rod of his mouth, and with the breath of his lips he shall kill the wicked. *Righteousness shall be the belt of his waist*, and faithfulness the belt of his loins.—Isaiah 11:1–5

This prophecy is about Jesus, the shoot from Jesse, the father of David. Isaiah tells us the actions of Jesus' life are righteous, equitable, and just, even as you would expect from someone who perfectly lived God's laws. But Isaiah tells us that Jesus' ability to live righteously had nothing to do with the law, instead coming because the Spirit of the Lord was upon him—the Spirit of wisdom.

BECOMING LIKE JESUS

Let's briefly recap: God never expelled us from his presence. Instead, we chose to hide because of our shame. Realizing that we already have the access we hoped our performance would buy us, we can leave behind the rules that trapped us in shame and led to our hiding. Having set aside the rules, we find a new way to live for God in the example of Jesus. He lived a perfectly righteous life not because of rules he memorized and worked hard at, but through an unbroken relationship with his Father through the Spirit of wisdom in which he did what he saw his Father doing and said what he heard his Father saying.

John the Baptist declared that he baptized with water for the repentance from sins but that the one coming after him—Jesus—would baptize with the Holy Spirit and with fire (Matthew 3:11). Jesus himself testified about this Holy Spirit, that the Father would send him to us after Jesus ascended to heaven. This promise was fulfilled on the day of Pentecost fifty days after Jesus' resurrection.

Every believer now has access to the Holy Spirit. In fact, he has been given to each one of us to seal us for salvation, as the Spirit of adoption, as our Comforter, and as the one who leads us into all truth, reminds us of all the things Jesus said, and does several other amazing things for us. Let's focus on just one of these things for now, that he is the Spirit of adoption, leading every believer to now relate to God as their Daddy.

John described this adoption in even more incredible terms, saying that we are "born of God" and "born again" (John 1:12–13 and 3:3–8, respectively). We truly are children of God. Jesus followed his Father's voice because he remained childlike. Now, because we are also children of God, we can do the same thing!

Let's also not forget that the Holy Spirit is still the Spirit of wisdom who came upon Jesus to lead him in all the ways of righteousness as well, and still again that this is the same Holy Spirit we have.

Do you hear what I'm telling you? I'm saying God's clear picture in the Bible is that we have every opportunity to relate to God the Father and the Holy Spirit in the same way Jesus did, leading to the same results! This includes a life of power where we see signs, wonders, and miracles, and it also includes a life of perfect blamelessness where we are learning to live the way Jesus did—in complete dependence on God—instead of by the rules we have always known.

This life leads to everything we have always pursued by trying to follow rules, only unlike the life with the rules, this life actually accomplishes what we hoped for! It conforms us to the image of Christ Jesus, where we do what is right simply because of who we are and whose we are, not because someone told us we have to. Doing right flows naturally out of our brand-new nature as sons and daughters of God, and whenever we don't know exactly what to do, the Spirit of wisdom comes right along to instruct us in the way we should go.

RETURNING TO THE GARDEN

I almost feel like a television paid-programming salesman, because I feel like I keep saying, "But wait! There's more!" But in this case it's true!

THE TREE OF LIFE

There is even more to this wonderful life God offers to us, and it shows us how truly this life is what God designed us for and designed for us from the very beginning.

Earlier when I quoted Isaiah's prophecy, I didn't finish it. The rest of it goes on to say:

> Righteousness shall be the belt of his waist, and faithfulness the belt of his loins. The wolf shall dwell with the lamb, and the leopard shall lie down with the young goat, and the calf and the lion and the fattened calf together; and a little child shall lead them. The cow and the bear shall graze; their young shall lie down together; and the lion shall eat straw like the ox. The nursing child shall play over the hole of the cobra, and the weaned child shall put his hand on the adder's den. They shall not hurt or destroy in all my holy mountain; for the earth shall be full of the knowledge of the LORD as the waters cover the sea.
> —Isaiah 11:5–9

That first verse you recognize because it was the last one I quoted before, but immediately after that comes this incredible series of verses that talk about prey and predator coming together so safely that even the smallest of children can play with them and lead them. This describes a returning to what the garden of Eden was like!

But please notice what led to this return to the garden: it's connected to something and doesn't just stand alone, because it is directly connected to Jesus being anointed with the Spirit of wisdom to bring righteousness and justice to a world in need. This is the work Jesus made possible and began through his sacrifice on the cross and resurrection from the dead. This is the work that continues through any person who lives by the Spirit of the Lord—the Spirit of wisdom!

God confirms this work of the Spirit to us in another way as well. When he removed Adam and Eve from the garden, he placed the cherubim and a flaming sword at the entrance of the garden to make sure they didn't try to return. Well, Hebrews 1:7 quotes the Psalms to say, "Of the angels he says, 'He makes his angels winds, and his ministers a flame of fire.'" This describes what God placed at the entrance to the garden—cherubim and a flaming sword, or winds and fire.

Think with me, where else in Scripture do we see winds and fire coming together? Yes! At the day of Pentecost when the Holy Spirit first came upon believers, baptizing them in power! We read what happened there where it says:

> When the day of Pentecost arrived, they were all together in one place. And suddenly there came from heaven a sound like a mighty rushing wind, and it filled the entire house where they were sitting. And divided tongues as of fire appeared to them and rested on each one of them. And they were all filled with the Holy Spirit and began to speak in other tongues as the Spirit gave them utterance.—Acts 2:1–4

When the Holy Spirit came upon believers—the same Spirit by whom Jesus had the wisdom to live righteously and begin leading the world back toward the garden—he manifested to them as wind and fire. The very same two things that once guarded the entrance to the garden now fell upon all the believers as a sign that we may enter into life as it was in the beginning.

Why would God let us back into the garden life? Because the reason he forced them to leave had nothing to do with punishment and everything to do with protection. He made them leave to keep them from eating from the tree of life, the tree that would have given them a system to live by without rules, full of wisdom gained through relationship with God our Father. Now that Jesus had fulfilled the law and the prophets, he had made the way for us to sever ties with Adam's tree (family tree and the tree of the knowledge of good and evil) to partake of God's tree (family tree and the tree of life).

Can you see how this all works together? It was God's plan from the very beginning to redeem us from Adam's foolish choice. He did it all along while still honoring the dominion he gave to humankind by eventually giving a law that defined good and evil, then sending his Son to fulfill that law and provide a way for us to return to the tree of life that was offered to us so long ago.

Oh, and one last tidbit just for fun. Proverbs tells us, "[Wisdom] is a tree of life to those who lay hold of her; those who hold her fast are called blessed" (3:18). It's just another sign from God calling us to embrace what he offers us through the Spirit we already have—the Spirit of wisdom and adoption—and to live life in the image of God, just the way Jesus did.

SECTION TWO:
THE PROCESS

Chapter 9

PERMISSION TO CHANGE

Becoming like God means we have to change. Change means we need to count the cost of leaving the life we are used to. But change also means embracing a life so incredible that it can only be described as being like God. In this new life, we are no longer concerned with the past, but instead with our amazing future with Jesus.

Admittedly, one of the reasons I chose the college I attended was because it was just far enough away from my family to let me discover myself in a way I felt I hadn't yet been able to. Some of the reasons for this were silly—like wanting to try new foods without being teased by a family that had always known me to be picky—but even silly reasons like this felt legitimate.

Those were some of my plans for my time at college, but God had plans for me there too—plans to catch me up into a prayer movement that had begun the previous year. I encountered God in a way I never had before, and those encounters changed me. I began to find myself in ways I never expected, and in ways that were certainly more wonderful than trying new foods.

At college, I had a prayer chapel in my dorm building and an independent schedule. I established a habit of praying at 10 p.m. almost every night. Every Friday I went to, and eventually helped lead, a five-hour prayer meeting. As you can imagine, a prayer meeting that long is only possible if God shows up. If he isn't there, everyone would be bored and at a loss for words within the first hour. I met God in that place of prayer, and he changed me.

But no one at home had been along for the journey. Every break from school, I would come home to my amazing, supportive Christian family, and they would treat me the same as they always had. And of course they would; there was no reason for them not to. What I experienced in those times, however, was a pull to return to the man who left for school and abandon the man who had come home from school. I felt pressure—not in any overt way from my family, but still very real—to leave behind the change God had worked in my life and become the person I had always been.

AN HONEST QUESTION

God wants to make us like him, and you can figure out on your own that this means we're going to go through quite a bit of change during this process. Not all change is pleasant, though, and even some changes that seem like no-brainers can be difficult to accept.

One story from Jesus' earthly ministry shows us some things that can help us with this:

> After this there was a feast of the Jews, and Jesus went up to Jerusalem. Now there is in Jerusalem by the Sheep Gate a pool, in Aramaic called Bethesda, which has five roofed colonnades. In these lay a multitude of invalids—blind, lame, and paralyzed. One man was there who had been an invalid for thirty-eight years. When Jesus saw him lying there and knew that he had already been there a long time, he said to him, "Do you want to be healed?" The sick man answered him, "Sir, I have no one to

put me into the pool when the water is stirred up, and while I am going another steps down before me." Jesus said to him, "Get up, take up your bed, and walk." And at once the man was healed, and he took up his bed and walked.—John 5:1–9

This is a truly remarkable story, if for no other reason than that it shows us how mind-boggling miracles were happening in Israel on a somewhat regular basis. Somehow, God appointed that this pool would become a place of healing; every so often he sent an angel who would stir up the water, and whoever jumped in first would be healed of their affliction.

Jesus came to this place during a particular Jewish feast, and of the multitude who were there, one man stood out to him. Somehow he knew this man had been there for a long time. Maybe he had seen him there before, maybe even many times, or maybe it was a prophetic knowing. How Jesus knew about this man doesn't really matter. What does matter is the question Jesus asked him: "Do you want to be healed?"

We might think this is rather a dumb question, or at least we would if anyone other than Jesus were asking it. The man was so bad off that he had lived in the company of beggars, invalids, and hopeless cases for nearly four decades. Can you imagine the atmosphere that would fill a place like that? Can you imagine the smell? Sure, it's a pool of water, but there's a multitude of people who need help getting around gathered around it. You can't imagine they had convenient bathrooms nearby with handicap access and showers available. The pool couldn't possibly have been even close to anything we would want to touch.

Take that physical description of the place and add to it the spiritual dynamic that most Jews of that day would have considered every person near that pool to be cursed by God. That's how they would have interpreted those peoples' afflictions and maladies. It was a room full of spiritually unclean people, and that wasn't just how the outside world thought of them; it would have been how they thought of themselves as well.

Obviously, this place wasn't exactly somewhere most people would enjoy going. It would have been a congregation of some of the most unpolished, depressed, broken, outcast, and degraded people you could find in all of Israel. Now, I don't know if you've spent much time with people who fit this kind of description, but in general they aren't fun to be around. They tend to create an atmosphere around themselves that reinforces what they believe about themselves (as we all do).

Despite all that, Jesus considers it an honest question to ask this man whether he wants to be healed. Did he want the one thing he needed that would enable him to leave that pool and find a real home?

There are a number of reasons why the man might not have wanted to get well. He had lived as a beggar for so long that being well would mean he couldn't beg anymore. He would have to go to work for perhaps the first time in his life and make a living by entering the competitive business world. What's more, he might have never learned a trade. Begging might have been the most useful skill he had. It might actually have required a lot of work for him to adjust to a life of being well.

COUNTING THE COST

Changing his situation was going to cost him, and Jesus wanted to know if he was truly willing to pay that cost. Change in our lives will also always have a cost. I once sat down with a couple to help prepare them for getting married. In the course of our discussions, I began telling them about the cost of marriage. I asked them, "Are you willing to give what marriage requires? Because the cost is everything; it costs your life. When you are single, you can do whatever you want, but as soon as you make those vows, you do not belong to yourself anymore."

Why would I have such a sobering conversation with people who are about to embark on one of the most joyous transitions we can take? It's because too many couples shipwreck their marriages because either no one taught them the cost or they failed to accurately understand it until it was too late and they found they weren't willing to give that much.

So let's be up front about the cost of following Jesus. It costs you everything, and I mean absolutely everything. It means you consider your old life to be dead, buried, and rotting in the ground, completely out of reach to you anymore. This is the cost of being healed and made whole. Whatever he requires of us, we give it.

In my experience, this cost usually translates into a willingness to forgive those who hurt you, to stay rooted where God puts you even when the journey is hard and long, and to cultivate both a faith and a love that are bigger than your fears. Those three things are what lead to success in God's eyes.

But the offer God gives us is real life, a life of genuine identity, becoming everything he created us to be. It means becoming like God himself! It means living with supernatural power, with freedom in our souls so tangible that we can't help but be filled with peace and joy every day. God offers love—true love—that casts out all fear, comforts every hurt, and draws nearest every time we need it most. He gives us protection, wholeness, clarity of thought and quietness of mind, victory over sin, intimacy with his heart, revelation of his mind, and the presence of his Spirit.

And that's just the beginning. Words can't even begin to describe what God offers to us, and of course the cost pales in comparison. But we still must be willing to pay it, so we need to know what it is.

OPPOSITION TO CHANGE

The man at the pool knew his answer to Jesus' question. He wanted to be made well, so of course Jesus healed him. He told him to take up his mat and go home. There was only one problem. It was the Sabbath, which meant it wasn't long before this poor man who had just been healed fell into trouble with the rule police—the Pharisees. They told him it was against Jewish law for him to carry his bed on the Sabbath.

His reply was simple: "The man who healed me is the one who told me to carry it" (John 5:11, my paraphrase). He knew instinctively that whoever had the power to heal him had more authority than the Pharisee's rules, but that didn't keep him out of trouble.

The ultimate root of the problem was that, while the afflicted man had been healed of what ailed him, the Pharisees were still in need of healing and didn't know it. Jesus would have healed them, but they didn't realize they were sick. Similarly, there are times when God sets us free from things or brings change into our lives, but the people who are still stuck don't like it. It makes them uncomfortable because it challenges all the defenses they have created for themselves as excuses for their dysfunction.

So what do we do when the people around us don't know how to relate to a new us? Well, you have three choices.

First, you can stay put and make them deal with the change in your life, hoping that it gives them time to adjust. In my family's case, this worked (because they're amazing, and because we communicated), but in many cases it doesn't. One of the biggest hurdles to people quitting chemical addictions is the need to get new friends. They think they are strong enough to keep the same friends they partied with and stay clean and sober, but almost no one can handle that. When God brings change in your life, it very well may bring a similar situation to you where you need to decide between the life you had and the life you want.

Second, you can try to become a leader who helps others into change. This is tricky for me to talk about because it depends so greatly on someone's personality. Some can stand in a group and lead them while they change. Others will need to go through the whole process until they really complete the change God has worked in them before they would have the confidence to try to lead others. Some would never have interest in being a leader anyway. The only word I can say here is a word of caution: don't overestimate your ability to retain the change in your life while trying to lead your friends into their own encounters with God. It's better to keep the change God's working in you than to keep your old group of friends.

Third, you can find new friends who expect you to change. This, honestly, is going to be the easiest and healthiest choice for most people in the long run. When the people who are most influential in your life expect you to change and you expect them to change, you can learn to cheer each other on as God steps you closer to his image. You can call out the best in each other and celebrate victories. You can seek God together and become a part of each other's transformations. It becomes a family-like community where love flourishes, commitment deepens, and the process of becoming like God can accelerate.

That doesn't mean a new group of friends will be perfect. Remember, you are all on the journey of becoming perfected, so no one is perfect yet, which means there will still be conflicts from time to time and things that need to be worked through. However, it is certainly easier to pursue God alongside others who are doing the same thing and have the same heart than it is to be alone in a group that won't go with you.

THE PROCESS OF CHANGE

Whether or not you find a group of people so you can pursue God's changing work in your life together, it's necessary to understand how God works change in our lives. If we don't have vision for how God does work in us, then it's all too easy to return to the lists of rules and our own efforts at keeping them as evidence of our changed lives. But as I keep saying, that kind of work is only human effort, which can only produce human results, while God is calling us to become supernaturally transformed into something the world has never seen.

At the risk of sounding cliché, here are the five steps God leads us through to transform us into his image:

Step One: Believe the Gospel

It should go without saying that we'll never have transformed lives until God enters the picture. The good news is that all Christians have already taken this step or they wouldn't be Christians. We believe Jesus died for our sins and rose again to give us life everlasting with him.

Step Two: Get Adopted

This actually happens at the exact same moment as Step One. One is the result of the other, or maybe better put, it's simply a different way of defining our salvation. Taking Jesus as our Savior by faith also means taking God as our Father. You can't have one without the other. So, assuming you are a Christian, congratulations on already completing the first two steps toward your transformed life!

Step Three: Receive Discipline

Hebrews 12:7 promises us that being a child of God means he will discipline us, which doesn't often make us think happy thoughts. However, it's helpful for us to consider the means and purpose of God's discipline. Moses once explained this for us in saying this to Israel:

> "And [God] humbled you and let you hunger and fed you with manna, which you did not know, nor did your fathers know, that he might make you know that man does not live by bread alone, but man lives by every word that comes from the mouth of the LORD. ... Know then in your heart that, as a man disciplines his son, the LORD your God disciplines you."—Deuteronomy 8:3–5

God's method of discipline was not sickness, death, destruction, or disaster; it was the daily practice by which he proved his word is trustworthy, giving manna just as he promised. Though every household was bankrupt of food at night, he met their need the following morning every day for forty years. The purpose of this was to teach them to trust his words, which included obeying his commands, but also included the promise that he would deliver a land filled with hostile giants and a multitude of strong nations into their hands. Without having faith in God's words, Israel would never enter the Promised Land.

That was why God, as a good father, trained them through discipline to live by his words instead of by their circumstances. God's discipline in our lives will be equally gentle and accomplish the same purpose, establishing trust and faith that his words are true so we will believe and live by them.

Step Four: Become Free

Jesus prays in John 17:17, "Sanctify them in the truth; your word is truth." He also said, "If you abide in my word, you are truly my disciples, and you will know the truth, and the truth will set you free" (John 8:31–32). This is the exact process we are talking about—living in his words so we know the truth, which then sets us free. It's interesting that God's words result in two things: 1) us being set apart completely unto him, and 2) us becoming free. Isn't it wonderful to see the very thing that brings us closer to him also sets us free from the things that would control us and cause us to sin?

Step Five: Be Transformed

It's no wonder, then, that Romans 12:2 says, "Do not be conformed to this world, but be transformed by the renewal of your mind." Perhaps it's easier for us to read this verse and apply it backward—trying to be transformed in our actions first so that we can think differently about ourselves and earn a closer relationship with God—but that's not what it says. We can try to transform our lives all we want, but there's only one way it's going to happen—by renewing our minds.

That means to make our minds new, to think in a new way. But how are we going to do that? By now the answer is clear. We learn to think a new way by listening to the truth of what God says to us. We regularly bathe in his view of us and become increasingly cleansed from who the world, our past, or any other voice says we are or ought to be. The result of this is that we no longer resemble the world around us, but instead live the transformed lives we always desired but could never attain through our own efforts.

Paul wrote about this in a different way, saying:

> Husbands, love your wives, as Christ loved the church and gave himself up for her, that he might sanctify her, having cleansed her by the washing of water with the word, so that he might present

the church to himself in splendor, without spot or wrinkle or any such thing, that she might be holy and without blemish.—Ephesians 5:25–27

The apostle directly tells us that Jesus' method for purifying us, setting us apart to himself, and preparing us to be a perfect Bride for him is his words. He speaks to us. He washes us in his words.

Now I know what some of you are thinking, but his words are not angry words of correction. In fact, much of the time his words aren't about us at all. He will speak to us about himself because he knows the power of when we truly get a revelation of who he is.

THE PROCESS IN SKIN

God's process of transformation simply looks like this: demonstrating faithfulness to us to build trust so that when he speaks we believe him. Then, because we believe him, he can speak to us truths that set us free from the lies we believe about him, ourselves, or the world around us that have held us back from becoming who he created us to be.

One time the Lord did this very thing in me while I was simply mowing my lawn. I don't remember thinking about anything in particular while I walked back and forth across the grass, but God's presence interrupted my task and I felt prompted to ask him a particular question. I followed the prompting and asked, "God, why did you make me?"

I was expecting to hear him say something of my purpose in life, something about the task I was born to accomplish. Instead of that, I heard his familiar voice answer, "I made you because I loved you even before you were born. You were born because of love."

Right away, the arguments against this rose up in my mind, which was just proof I believed lies about myself that wouldn't allow me to receive what God had said as truth. I knew what God had said, though, and I knew it was him who said it, so I skeptically said, "Really?"

He didn't force anything on me. There was no "Yes, it's the truth and you had better believe it, young man!" kind of answer from him. He simply asked me a question: "Well, why did you have children?"

I was undone. I know my own story, how God put love for my children in my heart as a teenager. It was a radical transformation that happened in a single moment that I remember clearly to this day. I knew very well how that love compelled me to have children—five of them—and that it was this love that caused them to be born.

His voice was so gentle. He then asked me, "If you created your children because of love, why would you think I am any different? Nathanael, you were born because I love you. I made you because I loved you even before you were born. My love caused you to be!"

I don't know whether any of my neighbors saw me wiping away my tears that day as I circled my yard, but I was wrecked. My lies unraveled, my heart swelled, and my spirit filled with the tangible light of his truth. I let go of the weight of obligation I had carried, thinking I was born for a task instead of a relationship. And not that there aren't things I am tasked with doing, like writing this book, but the relationship had to come first for me.

God's voice washed me in truth, setting me free and conforming me to his image. He spoke to me and made me more like him. Because I am his son, he disciplined me. Because he disciplined me, I trusted him. Because I trusted him, I believed his words. Because I believed his words, God transformed my life, making me more like him.

THE GLORY OF YOU

Paul wrote to us about this process more succinctly in 2 Corinthians 3:18: "And we all, with unveiled face, beholding the glory of the Lord, are being transformed into the same image from one degree of glory to another." What transforms us into his image is beholding his image! When we see his glory, it makes us glorious in the exact same way. When I saw God's love for me that was established before I could have possibly earned it, I was transformed to be able to love myself the same way. It changed me as a son, and in changing me as a son, it changed me as a husband, father, and friend. It made me better able to treat others with the love God had for me; it enabled me to live out the image of God he created me to carry.

But now—finally!—I get to begin making this message individual to you specifically. Up to this point I have been laying down foundational mindsets that make every individual identity possible. Now, congratulations, you have made it to the point where I can talk about you in all your amazingness.

In fact, I don't just *get* to talk about you specifically; I *have* to, because God is so big that no one person could become the fullness of his image. God showed this to me in the sunrise I wrote about in the foreword of this book, when the colors spread from horizon to horizon and God said every Christian is like one pixel in a picture of that sunrise.

So here's where this brings us—when God reveals himself to someone, it transforms them into his image, yet no single one of us can become his entire image. It takes all of us together being the one part of his image, like billions of puzzle pieces all coming together to form the composite image of God. One revelation from God shapes us more and more into that pixel, or into that precious stone. Each encounter with God changes us into more of who he made us to be.

And God knows the power of when we encounter him. He designed us that way, after all. So he isn't going to reveal himself to you in the same way that he will reveal himself to me. He will only reveal himself to you in the way that will conform you to the identity he created uniquely for you, the identity you were born to become, the image of God you were destined to be.

Ah, and I wish I could tell you this next part in person so you could see the look in my eyes and hear the passion in my voice. The truth you just read shows just how incredibly, unspeakably, powerfully important you are, because you—yes, you—are a unique revelation of God to this world. Your one-of-a-kind identity is handcrafted by God himself to reveal him to the world in a way that only you can. This is the amazing beauty of being made in the image of God. It has everything to do with how it takes all of us to comprise the full image of God, and it has everything to do with how each and every one of us is a unique revelation of God within that magnificent whole.

That means if I meet you on the street, I don't just value you because you are generically made in God's image. No, I deeply honor you because I know you carry a secret about God that I can experience only through, from, and in relationship with you! This is why I am writing this book. It's because I need you to become you! The world needs you to become you! And most of all, you need you to become you!

Well, there is where my language fails me, because all "need" aside, no one's needs matter when it comes to you becoming you. Sure, the needs are true somewhere in this equation, but what matters far, far more is that becoming you is truly what you were created for. It's what will fulfill you, satisfy you, and make you feel like you are thriving in life, truly alive. It's what will let you wake up in the morning and say, "I know why I'm alive!" And it only comes through those encounters with God in which he reveals himself to you in the way that's unique to you, transforming you into his image from glory to glory.

BEGINNING TO DREAM

Let's bring all this together now. Becoming like God is going to require us to change. Sometimes this change is uncomfortable, so we should count the cost. However, it's always worth it, especially when we can go through it with a group of people who come alongside us to cheer us on. After all, the change God brings us through is never based on rules and always based on encountering him and hearing his voice.

Take another look at that last sentence there. Up to this point in this chapter, I hardly mentioned rules at all, yet the whole chapter is about the process God takes us through to make us like him! Who would have thought you could have a life of following God that progressively moves toward being like him more and more, all without rules? That's life with wisdom and the tree of life in the Spirit of God.

But there's one more important contrast between these two lives that has so much to do with you becoming you. A relationship with God that's based on rules defaults to being focused on sin because it's all about what you're allowed to do, what you're not allowed to do, and whether you are living according to that prescription. It's a checklist focused on successes and failures, and because of the nature of how failure leads to shame, this life often becomes focused on failures much more than on successes. In that environment, there's barely even room for the question of who you were born to be because the concern is entirely about whether you conform to a standard of morality and not about whether you conform to the image of God.

When Christianity stops being about sin management and rule following, it has to turn its focus from the past onto the future, which requires us to begin dreaming about and envisioning the future God created us to make with him. You don't have to fill your mind with the rules. You're free. And when you're free, what will you do with your freedom?

Begin to dream, and let your dream flow out of the encounters you've had with God that revealed who you were born to be. Let your dreams be the natural by-product of who you are. Don't just conceptualize you—become you! Dream you, then live you!

Personalize your dream. Sew. Garden. Open some temporary housing for people getting out of jail, recovering addicts, or women and children from abusive homes. Rescue people from human trafficking. Solve the world's water or hunger problems. Discover the cure for AIDS and cancer. Be an amazing father or mother or husband or wife or friend. Become an indispensable employee at your work, or start your own company. Become the next Thomas Edison or Albert Einstein. Go after that job at the United Nations or take steps toward becoming president of the United States.

It doesn't matter what your dream is, but dream, and when you do, let God into the process. Let him inspire your dreams. Do what fits you and let God lead you.

Why would you need God to lead you when you're free to dream? The answer is easy, and it has nothing to do with him wanting to control you.

It's simply because almost all of the time, he believes in us more than we believe in ourselves. He has to lead us or we would eliminate ourselves, thinking that we're either disqualified or unqualified. But when we learn to think of ourselves the way he thinks of us, we can start to have the same dream for our lives that was in his heart even before we were born.

Once we have a dream, we have a destination. Once we have a destination, we have to face change because where we are is not where we are going, just as who we are is not who we are becoming. But if we have a culture that expects change, we also have a culture that celebrates and empowers destiny, whatever that looks like on an individual basis.

You can begin doing this even right now. Ask God to begin encountering you in a deeper way than he has in the past. Offer yourself to his hands to let him transform you. Invite him into your dreaming process. Let him speak to you so you can begin to think of yourself the way he thinks of you.

Then watch out, because your life is about to get more amazing than you ever thought possible.

Chapter 10

THE POWER OF YOUR VOICE

> As we discover who God made us to be, we also need to discover the tools he created to help us live our unique identity. Hands down, the most powerful tool he gives us is our voice. Knowing how powerful our voice is, where our voice comes from, and how to shape our words sets us on a straight path toward our incredible purpose.

Just over six years ago, my family moved to a town in rural Minnesota. There were only five of us at the time, and my children were ages two, one, and zero years old. Within the first two months of living in our new home, God told us we were going to plant a church in that city.

As we prayed into this word and for our city, God also started showing us many things about the spiritual atmosphere of our new home. My wife, Amy, and I had more encounters with the Lord and words from him about our city than I can count. Eventually, because of our hearts as parents, we wanted to bring our kids into the journey.

Our idea for how to easily involve them in praying for our city was to write declarations that we could make as a family. Every day we would gather as a family and go over the purpose and power of our declarations. We taught our kids to say, "My words are powerful and strong, and they make stuff happen!"

In the rapidly changing world that is life with young kids, we didn't keep our habit of daily family declarations for very long, but that phrase still sticks with us today. I can say, "My words are powerful …" and my children will finish the sentence for me. They understand at least something of how powerful our words are.

I'm surprised how strongly fellow believers sometimes respond when you talk to them about the power of their words. It's as though they think you're trying to push "magic words" on them like some deceptive form of witchcraft or superstition. In our naturalistic Western mindset, we sometimes don't give our words the credit they deserve, but let me share a story to illustrate how in other parts of the world, people believe very deeply in how powerful their words are.

A friend of mine served in the American military and told me about something he once witnessed while on duty in the Middle East during a combat tour there. At some point during his tour, he helped interrogate one of the enemy soldiers they had taken captive. Because the captive did not speak English, one of the local soldiers translated.

There was nothing noteworthy about the interrogation. Nothing unusual or bad had happened, though the captive was certainly uncooperative. Finally, the prisoner let loose in his own language, unleashing an angry tirade upon his American interrogator. Immediately, the local ally jumped up and began to beat the prisoner, so that my friend was forced to intervene for his enemy.

They left the room to regroup and my friend demanded to know what the man had said to provoke such a response. This local soldier began to interpret all the curses the enemy soldier had been declaring over this American. How interesting is it that while we are raised with, "Sticks and stones may break my bones, but words will never hurt me," this Arab man had quite a different understanding of the power words have?

THE POWER TO DIRECT

I could keep going on with story after story that would illustrate just how much words truly can affect us, but what I want to focus on specifically is the power of our own words toward our life. We can start with the following passage:

> If we put bits into the mouths of horses so that they obey us, we guide their whole bodies as well. Look at the ships also: though they are so large and are driven by strong winds, they are guided by a very small rudder wherever the will of the pilot directs. So also the tongue is a small member, yet it boasts of great things.
> —James 3:3–5

In these verses, James compares our tongues to the rudder of a ship. As someone who communicates regularly and publicly as part of my job, I understand that I need to be careful about overstating the importance of things. If I overemphasize everything, eventually people will stop listening. It's like only using exclamation points when you write or writing in all caps; you just can't communicate urgency or importance about every little thing you tell people. You have to choose your places to do that and make sure what you emphasize is truly worth the emphasis you give it.

James probably understood this as well, but whether he did or didn't, God certainly does. That's why I really pause carefully when I read a statement like what James has written for us here. I take the time to think about how important a ship's rudder is to that ship, or how important the bit and bridle is to a race horse or a war horse.

Perhaps you've seen the movie *Gladiator* with its opening scene depicting the final battle between the well-organized Roman army and the comparatively disorganized Germanic army. Russel Crowe's words ring in my mind as I think of that scene, his continuous mantra as he led his cavalry in their charge, shouting, "Stay together!" Could you imagine the difference if their cavalry rode horses with no bits or bridles? How would each soldier keep charge over his horse? How could the unit possibly attack with unity? They couldn't, which would lead to that entire division of the military becoming useless.

Or could you imagine how useless a ship would become with no rudder? The gallant Spanish Armada in all of its gilt splendor would have sat adrift. The great invasion of Troy would have amounted to nothing as unguidable ships crashed into each other or became so much elaborate driftwood on the Aegean Sea. Fancy Caribbean cruise ships wouldn't even get out of port!

That's how important a rudder is to a ship and how important a bit is to directing a horse, and those are the two things James chose to compare our tongue's power to direct our lives. This is the point James emphasized clearly as he wrote his letter, so we need to listen: our words direct our lives.

Our words direct our lives! I've heard it said somewhere that if I listen to the words coming out of your mouth, I can tell you where your life will go in the future. The book of Proverbs says it this way, "Death and life are in the power of the tongue, and those who love it will eat its fruits" (18:21). This is saying that those who talk a lot are creating their future for themselves, even to the drastic ends of life and death!

MATTERS OF THE HEART

This all makes a ton of sense, really, if you think about it. After all, our words are the truest witness of what we really believe. Jesus put it this way, "The good person out of the good treasure of his heart produces good, and the evil person out of his evil treasure produces evil, for out of the abundance of the heart his mouth speaks" (Luke 6:45). What comes out of our mouth ultimately reveals what is hidden in our heart.

Why would it matter what is hidden in our heart? How is that supposed to predict the path our life takes? It matters because our heart hides what we truly believe. The story of the twelve spies perfectly shows us not just how much what we believe matters, but also how our words are important. I'll summarize most of the story.

After leading the nation of Israel out of slavery in Egypt, Moses took the people right up to the edge of the Promised Land. This was the territory God promised to their forefathers Abraham, Isaac, and Jacob. God had told Israel it was time to take possession of the promise and that he would be with them the whole way to drive out every nation and people who already lived in the land.

Finding themselves right on the edge of their destiny, Moses sent twelve spies into the land. He chose one man from each tribe, telling them to search out the land to discover the strengths and weaknesses of the land and the people who lived there, and to bring back fruit if they could.

The spies returned to tell Israel that the land was indeed very good, demonstrating just how good it was by showing them a cluster of grapes so large that it took two men to carry it. But ten of the spies also told the people how terribly large and strong the people of the land were. They talked about how thick and tall the walls around the cities were. They didn't just paint a picture of hopelessness; they directly told everyone it was hopeless and that it would have been better for them to have all stayed enslaved in Egypt.

That's what ten of the spies said, but two gave a different report. They had also seen the giants in the land and the powerful cities they would have to overcome, but they believed their God was bigger and stronger, so they said, "We can do it! Our God will deliver them into our hands!" But it was no use. The hearts of the people melted in fear because of the report the ten had given. They spoke of killing Moses and returning to Egypt, until God broke in.

God's presence fell in power upon the assembly so that the leaders fell on their faces before him. God rebuked the people for their faithless fear and issued this profound sentence:

> "As I live, declares the Lord, what you have said in my hearing I will do to you: your dead bodies shall fall in this wilderness, and of all your number listed in the census from twenty years old and upward, who have grumbled against me, not one shall

come into the land where I swore that I would make you dwell, except Caleb the son of Jephunneh and Joshua the son of Nun."
—Numbers 14:28–30

What's important for us to see in this true story is that Joshua and Caleb saw the exact same things as the other ten spies, yet they looked at them in a completely different way. Their interpretation was rooted in faith that God would do good to them, but the ten's interpretation was rooted in faith that doom waited for them. Ultimately, what the ten had faith for is what happened to them (doom) and what the two had faith for is what happened for them (they conquered and possessed the land).

Henry Ford once said, "Whether you think you can, or think you can't—you're right."[8] Ten spies thought they couldn't take possession of the land, so they couldn't. Two spies thought they could take possession of the land, knowing God was with them, so they could. The important word in those statements is the smallest: *so*. The thoughts in their hearts were the very reason they either could or couldn't do what was before them. Their inner reality created their external one.

So often we think that our external reality, our circumstances, are more powerful than the reality within us, but that's all a lie. God is with us, which means there is nothing we cannot overcome, including the voices inside us that seek to keep us small and insignificant, trapped in the slavery of life apart from our created purpose and identity.

CULTIVATING FAITH FOR GOOD

If our words direct our life and our heart produces our words, then the way to direct our life toward our identity, purpose, and dreams is to intentionally tend our faith. We have to take care of our inner world by cultivating faith that good things are going to happen for us.

The main obstacle to this is that Satan and his minions, not to give them too much credit, seem to know our destiny before we do and work overtime to bury us in insecurities and failures that make us think we're crippled in the very areas where we are created to run. Thankfully, first, they are already defeated and deception is their only hope. And thankfully, second, they are terribly impatient, while our God is faithful to stay with us to the end of the process, continually redeeming the past to make an even more glorious future.

I can't begin to emphasize how important it is to have faith for good. Expecting good things from God is absolutely necessary or we can never become who we were created to be. In fact, expecting good from God is so important that faith isn't even faith without it.

The most famous chapter in the Bible on the subject of faith is Hebrews 11, often called the Hall of Faith because it recounts the stories of many heroes and heroines of faith. Near the beginning of that chapter we find this nugget: "And without faith it is impossible to please [God], for whoever would draw near to God must believe that he exists and that he rewards those who seek him" (Hebrews 11:6).

I think all of us reading this book know we have a vested interest in pleasing God, so the first words of this verse definitely jump out at us. Wow, it's impossible to please God without faith? Well, then, I guess I'd better have faith! But that's a little ambiguous, isn't it? I mean, if the writer of Hebrews stopped there, would you understand how to live in a way that showed you had the faith the writer was talking about?

Thankfully, the author didn't stop there, continuing on to say, "For whoever would draw near to God must believe that he exists and that he rewards those who seek him." The first part of this is a bit of a no-brainer. If you want to please God, you have to actually believe he exists. It does go a little deeper than this, however, because the literal translation here would be, "For those who would draw near to God must believe that *he is*." This is a direct reference to the only name God gave himself, "I Am." I have long believed this is not just a name to declare his self-existence, his sole claim to being the Creator of all things, but that it is a mystery—an invitation to explore who and what he is. It's an unfinished sentence, a question that begs an answer that can only be discovered through relationship.

The second part is our main focus here, though, where it says, "And that he rewards those who seek him." This is the Bible directly telling us that if we are going to draw near to God, we absolutely have to believe he will reward us for seeking him. In other words, you can't draw near to God without believing for blessing.

This is a foundational verse for how I walk out my faith, which began when I believed God would reward me with salvation if I accepted Jesus as my Savior. That was the first step of faith in my life. I believed that because of Jesus I would go to heaven when I died instead of hell. That definitely qualifies as a great reward for seeking God!

Clearly, though, we can search the Scriptures and find many more ways God rewarded people who sought him. David famously lists several of them in Psalm 103, declaring, "Bless the Lord, O my soul, and forget not all his benefits" (v. 2). He knew that following God invited a lengthy list of benefits into his life, and he exhorted his soul to never forget them.

You could say with complete honesty that this entire book came from simply believing that God's rewards don't stop at salvation and that I can discover more by reading his book, the Bible, because in reading the Bible I discovered that God made me to be like him. Now that is one incredible reward for seeking him!

The bottom line is that we need to believe God for good, and this is good news indeed for so many Christians. It's all too common for believers to be stuck in shame, which leads them to expect a lecture every time they draw near to God. It even leads to perverse understanding of what God's rewards might look like, interpreting deadly diseases like cancer or AIDS to be God's tools to refine our character.

Horrible misunderstandings like this stem from a belief that God is only interested in our character and morality, and not in making us entirely like him. Listen, God doesn't have cancer, so getting cancer won't make you like him. Sure, he can redeem a sickness to make it part of our process of becoming like him, but that doesn't make it his ordained tool for the job. Certainly, regardless of how God can redeem such terrible things in our lives, we can be sure they are never his will for us because they are not part of who he is so they are not his plan for who we are either.

Ultimately, why would God tell us in his Word that believing he rewards those who seek him is a required part of pleasing him? It's because he wants us to actually believe it! He wants us to know how good he is! Because, honestly, until we believe he's that good, we never will become that good. Because, as we've already talked about, it's as we see him that we become like him.

We have to not just believe that God is good but also believe for good from God. We have to believe his goodness means something tangible in our lives, that his goodness results in good actions that lead to us experiencing his goodness. It all makes complete sense. If he really is good, then we'll know it by our experience of good as we seek him. The closer to him we get, the more good we will encounter, because he is good.

If we will handle this issue in our head and heart, then we won't have to worry about what comes out of our mouth. If what's inside us expects good, we'll actually confess that belief in our words. Those words will then direct our lives toward the good we expect. We can begin proactively creating the future that belongs to our identity by declaring it years before we are able to begin living it.

DISCERNING THE VOICES WE HEAR

There's one more layer about our words that we need to cover. We have to understand some things about the other voices that surround us—how they can influence us, and how we can choose which voice will become the inspiration for our own.

In case this is new to you, let me tell you that we are not alone in this world. There is a spiritual realm full of angels and demons. I had a childhood friend who once tried to tell me that demons no longer exist, but I always wondered where he thought they went or what happened to them. No, they're still around, and they do try to influence us every day.

It's not like the classic television depiction, with an angel on one shoulder and a devil on the other, but these beings do have voices and they do speak to us. In fact, one of the angels' primary jobs is to be God's messengers to humankind. It's almost certain that you have heard angels' voices, often without realizing it.

Demonic voices are often easier to figure out when they're speaking to you, because they are the voices constantly trying to drag you down and convince you of how small and incapable you are. They are the voices that point out all your flaws and weaknesses, working to convince you to take up the worst parts of your past as your identity. They'll even try to convince you that all this degrading speech is God's voice convicting you of sin so you either pursue their condemning voices in your passion for God or run from God because you can't stand the condemnation and think it comes from him. It's a crafty scheme, don't you think?

However, as I mentioned earlier, our enemy's only weapon is deceit. He's been completely disarmed by Jesus' death and resurrection, so the only way he has power is if he can trick us into giving it to him. One of the main ways he does this is the scheme I just described—by accusing us until we believe things about ourselves that simply aren't true.

We need to be able to have full confidence that these voices I'm talking about really are demonic so we can learn to ignore them, resist them, get free from them, and fill our inner life with God's words instead. Two passages help make this issue clear. The first says:

> And I heard a loud voice in heaven, saying, "Now the salvation and the power and the kingdom of our God and the authority of his Christ have come, for the accuser of our brothers has been thrown down, who accuses them day and night before our God."—Revelation 12:10

This verse calls Satan "the accuser of our brothers" and tells us that this is his constant activity. He's the worst form of gossip magazine, continually finding dirt to fling, and you and I who believe in Jesus are the target of all his filthy accusations.

When we read this, we learn the nature of our foe. We understand he is interested in only one thing—tearing us down, even before our Father in heaven. When we understand this to be the nature of the devil, we can begin to draw a line in our heart against those internal voices that continually accuse us of things that bring shame. We can press the pause button when we recognize accusations ringing in our mind, and instead of receiving them as truth (because we recognize our own faults and, let's be honest, this voice always *feels* true) we can reject them. After all, it doesn't make sense to think, *Hmm, this thought is accusing me of something. The devil is always accusing me, so this voice in my head must be God.* No, when we recognize a demonic voice, we need to silence and ignore it, not receive it as our own thoughts or as the Holy Spirit.

It becomes easier to do this when we see the second passage, which says:

> "You are of your father the devil, and your will is to do your father's desires. He was a murderer from the beginning, and does not stand in the truth, because there is no truth in him. When he lies, he speaks out of his own character, for he is a liar and the father of lies."—John 8:44

These are Jesus' words telling us what the devil is like. He couldn't be more plain in what he says. The devil is a liar; that is his native language. It doesn't matter whether it comes out in English, Spanish, Mandarin, or Arabic—his native language is lying. In fact, he is such a liar that he is the father of lies.

KNOW YOUR ENEMY

Let's put together these two things that we now know about the devil. First, he constantly accuses us before God, and, second, he is an incessant liar. Well now, this makes a pretty picture for us, doesn't it? Can you see it?

The devil is a liar, and the words he does choose to say are accusations. That means his accusations aren't true! They're a pack of lies. All that garbage and dirt he digs up on you and me, it's all fake! Sure, there are maybe some half-truths woven in, or perhaps there are things that used to be true in there, but it's not true of us anymore because of who we have become in Christ.

So when you hear voices of accusation in your heart or in your mind, I know it may sound an awful lot like your own thoughts, or it may sound an awful lot like the Holy Spirit's voice, but it's not. That's not the way your loving Father and big brother Jesus speak to you. It's a demonic voice speaking to you, trying to get you to buy into its lies so it can influence you away from God's created purpose for your life—to make you like him.

If a demon can get you to believe that you are trapped in sin, that you are compelled by nature to lie, cheat, lust, manipulate, gossip, lose your temper, or whatever, then it just put a roadblock between you and the image God created you to become. Or if a demon can get you to believe that you are unloved, disfavored, chronically poor, unhealthy, unworthy, insignificant, or shameful, that is just its lie to keep you from living the identity God created just for you.

Now, I need to make a clarification about one point, because I know some reading this will ask this question. If you hear demonic voices, that doesn't make you demon possessed; it makes you human. Everyone hears these voices. I say it again—*everyone* hears these voices. Everyone! I hear them. My wife hears them. My pastor friends hear them. My kids hear them. Everyone hears them, and it's not a shameful thing; it's a human thing.

In fact, it has nothing to do with you at all and everything to do with them. I mean, what are they supposed to do, stop talking and lying and deceiving and destroying? Or where are they going to go, to some other planet or realm without humans, who are the crown of God's creation and object of his love? They're just going to leave us alone? Really? Or is it just those super evil people who worship Satan and pursue the demonic who will hear demons? Why would demons hold themselves back in their own territory and only destroy the lives of people who invite it? Of course they'll go on the offensive to try to take more ground. They are always scheming for ways to deceive and destroy. It's their nature. It is who they are for them to try to keep you from becoming who you are. They want you to think you're like them, but you're not; you were made in the image of God!

I am convinced this is what drives the whole demonic kingdom—they are trying to make us in their image. Satan tried to enthrone himself above God, and he is still trying to do it by working to re-create the world according to his design and, in the process, destroying the one God made. The keystone to his perverted world is the same as in God's creation—to make something in his image. He is continually trying to make us like him. This issue really does come down to the question, "Who's your daddy?" Are you like your father, the devil, or are you like your Father, God?

Jesus recognized that the Pharisees were like the devil, so in the same breath he said the devil was their father. But that isn't who you are. You chose to put your faith in Jesus Christ, and when you did he gave you the Spirit of adoption. There's no question, not even any concern, about who your Father is. You belong to God. You bear his name. You are his child and you are continually being made more perfectly into his image.

BUILD YOUR THOUGHTS ON PURPOSE

This is why we need to "take every thought captive to obey Christ" (2 Corinthians 10:5). We captivate our thoughts so we don't end up wandering down a road of shame and condemnation because we listened to those lying, accusing voices trying to shape us into their evil image.

Instead, we impregnate our thoughts with what God has declared over us. We meditate on his words so they become a light to the path of our life. We take Paul's advice:

> Finally, brothers, whatever is true, whatever is honorable, whatever is just, whatever is pure, whatever is lovely, whatever is commendable, if there is any excellence, if there is anything worthy of praise, think about these things.—Philippians 4:8

And, of course, we draw near to God so we encounter him in ways that become profound for the very reason that they wash away how we used to think about ourselves, revealing through experience what God has always known to be true about us. These are the thoughts we place as the foundation for our lives, the ones we live from.

Realizing the truth about those accusing thoughts we are all so familiar with is incredibly empowering. This truth gives us the power to overcome our past. The truth is, we never were disqualified. The truth is, we never sinned too much. And while I am certainly not discounting or lessening the evil of what some of us have been through, the truth still is that we never were abused too harshly or too deeply that God cannot redeem us and establish us in who we were born to be.

Our past does not define our future. How we did things in the past can change right now. We just need to take responsibility for our life, beginning with the voices we allow to influence us. The voices we listen to feed what we keep in our heart, out of our heart our mouth speaks, and our words direct our lives. Each one of us can become everything we were born to be, and it starts with who you listen to.

But don't forget where this all began, talking about the importance of our words. I expect that if you address the root of your words, the fruit will almost certainly come along in due time. However, the words we say are still words we choose to say. Begin today to choose carefully words that bring life to your future and direct you toward what God has for you. Listen carefully to what you have to say both internally and externally, then catch the negative and turn it around.

"Keep your heart with all vigilance, for from it flow the springs of life" (Proverbs 4:23). Guard against demonic voices and instead treasure God's words. Cultivate belief in what God says about you. Declare what God says about you. Then walk in the way your words direct you.[9]

As you empower God's voice in your life, living by what he says about you, may you flourish! May your life move from glory to glory!

Chapter 11

DEEP ROOTS

> When God speaks his promise over our lives, it almost always feels urgent. We sense that his promise could happen at any moment! The reality, however, is that time is often the most important ingredient to our identity. We can't arrive overnight, but waiting is worth it. Articulating a clear vision is the key to sustaining our faith as we wait for God's promises.

My friend spoke to a group of about twenty college students packed into my dorm's prayer chapel. It was Friday night and we were in the middle of our weekly prayer meeting. We listened as he exhorted us from the parable of the persistent widow. This was the story Jesus told about a woman who repeatedly came before an unrighteous judge to receive justice. Finally, the judge relented, not for the sake of doing what was right, but because he recognized the woman would wear him out.

My friend reminded us that the point of Jesus' story is that it teaches us something important about prayer—that sometimes we must be unrelenting, knowing that God will surely bring justice to our situation, even if at times we must endure. Then he gave us a surprising assignment: "I want each of us in here tonight to ask God to give us one or two things he wants us to not leave him alone about until he gives them to us."

I was intrigued and followed his instructions. God gave me two things to be steadfast about in my prayers that night, and one of them was that I would pray every day that God would give me my wife until he did. It wasn't until two years later that I was finally engaged to be married, and shortly after that was married. Nearly every day during those two years, I remained faithful to what I felt God told me to do. I prayed that he would give me my wife.

Now, "praying" isn't exactly the right word for what I did all the time. "Complaining" or "whining" might be a better description for some of those times because, I admit, I desperately wanted to be married. God miraculously put a love for my own wife and kids into my heart as a teenager and that love burned to find the person it belonged to. But God's faithfulness inspired mine. He confirmed his promise to me over and over again to embolden my prayers and keep me from losing heart.

THE CONTEXT SAYS WHAT?!

Maybe you have experienced something similar to this in your life, where God has promised something to you, and it felt like it could happen at any moment, but it didn't. You waited and waited and perhaps began to wonder if God forgot his promise, or, because you know he didn't, you wondered if you misheard him. Only then, right when you were about to give up hope, he confirmed the promise again in some unmistakable way.

If you haven't had this kind of experience yet, you most likely will as you discover and learn to live your identity. So what is this, exactly? Why does it seem God works this way?

Well, several times during my waiting period, well-intentioned friends would quote Psalm 37:4: "Delight yourself in the Lord, and he will give you the desires of your heart." They meant this to encourage me, looking in their own way to confirm that since I delighted in the Lord and desired a wife, then surely God would give me a wife. I think, at my school, all of us as single college students longing to be married mutually comforted ourselves with this verse.

It wasn't until years later that I learned the context around this verse. I've said this before, but it's worth repeating: context is everything when you want to understand the Bible (or any communication, for that matter). You have to understand the small part of what is said by looking at how it fits within the bigger picture around it.

The context for this verse promising that God would give me the desires of my heart goes like this:

> Fret not yourself because of evildoers; be not envious of wrongdoers! For they will soon fade like the grass and wither like the green herb. *Trust* in the LORD, and do good; *dwell* in the land and *befriend faithfulness*. Delight yourself in the LORD, and he will give you the desires of your heart. *Commit* your way to the LORD; *trust* in him, and he will act. He will bring forth your righteousness as the light and your justice as the noonday. *Be still* before the LORD and *wait patiently* for him; fret not yourself over the one who prospers in his way, over the man who carries out evil devices. … For the evildoers shall be cut off, but those who *wait* for the LORD shall inherit the land.—Psalm 37:1–9

Trust. Dwell. Befriend faithfulness. Commit. Trust. Be still. Wait patiently. Wait.

Those words are the context for "Delight yourself in the LORD, and he will give you the desires of your heart." Twice these verses tell us to trust. Twice they tell us to wait, and wait patiently. Be still. Dwell, put down roots, don't move. Make faithfulness your intimate friend. Commit.

Commit. Seriously, that's a sobering word, isn't it? Maybe commitment isn't so scary if we understand what we're committing to, but this is a commitment where we don't really know what it means. If we commit our way to the Lord, we are giving him control. We're saying yes to him unreservedly, promising to not grab the steering wheel of our life again because we grew impatient during the process.

That's why it said to trust—twice. If we completely understood the process, why would we have to trust? And trust is an interesting word when you combine it with "wait patiently." That means you should probably secure your trust deep into your heart because you might need to hold onto that trust for a long time without seeing any sign your trust will be rewarded.

This is the casing that surrounds the promise in the middle, like a precious stone set among all these other commands. But here is what I can tell you about this passage—truly the most powerful words are at the beginning of the promise: "Delight yourself in the Lord."

If you do this, as you gaze on the Lord in your delight, you will discover how good he is. You'll learn how deep is his love, how lavish is his mercy, how rich is his grace, how nearer than a heartbeat is his Spirit, and how indescribable is his presence. You'll discover the very character of who God is, and this is the effect it will bring: you'll trust even more. You'll know that if God promised something to you, he's good for it and you won't wait forever. And you'll know that as you continue standing before him, he will lead you in whatever direction you need to go to find the promise's fulfillment.

More than that, the very act of delighting yourself in the Lord forces us to choose to stay vulnerable. Otherwise we could wall off our heart from feeling the wait or the burden of our trust, but if we wall off our heart from those difficult things, we will also wall off our heart from delighting in God. You cannot selectively wall off yourself from vulnerability or choose which part of your heart to harden. You cannot harden one part without affecting the rest.

But if you stay vulnerable to God, you also open the rest of yourself to him. You place yourself at the focus of his love, even when it comes to comfort the waiting that has become hard. You root yourself in the very place where the promise will come, having built the character necessary for the promise in the very act of steadfastly committing yourself to faithfulness while delighting in him.

TRIALS OF FAITH

Okay, now take a deep breath. What you just read probably didn't sound like good news. I'm sorry if it felt that way; genuinely, I am. Waiting isn't fun. I know from personal experience. But I love an insight about waiting that Kris Vallotton teaches in regard to sexual purity. He says the reason we have a sex drive years before we can righteously satisfy it is so that the gift we give our spouse has value. The value comes from the cost we spent during the years of waiting.[10]

It's almost as though God offers us a promise of incredible value but then takes us through a process to help us understand just how valuable that promise really is. This process isn't some way for us to pay the value of the promise or to earn it in any way. We could never do that. But the determination we are forced to grow when we face the choice to keep waiting or to give up builds a value within us for the promise God has given us until the promise is as important to us as it is to him.

There's a lot more for us to receive in this process, however, than just a sense of value for the promise God has given us. In fact, you might say what he gives us through this process is literally without limit. Let me walk you through what this can look like in real-life terms.

It starts when God speaks to you. You encounter him, whether powerfully or subtly, but he's spoken to you either directly or through a prophetic word someone gave you. That's when it happens. Life begins to look even more opposite to the word God spoke to you than before he spoke it to you. I have seen this look like a weekend at church where person after person tells me God is releasing new levels of provision over my life, then the following week my dishwasher breaks or my basement floods. These are things that have actually happened to me, and yes, I did wonder how in the world those events could possibly be God releasing the provision my family desperately needed at that time.

If this sort of thing has happened to you, I need to tell you something important: *this is normal!* Our answer to this mystery starts with James 1:2–4:

> Count it all joy, my brothers, when you meet trials of various kinds, for you know that the testing of your faith produces steadfastness. And let steadfastness have its full effect, that you may be perfect and complete, lacking in nothing.

Do you see what the trials we face are all about? They are a testing of our faith. Now, according to Hebrews 11:1, faith is being confident of what we can't see. This means we are starting to form a description for the process of God's promises, which goes as follows:

First, God leads you somewhere or tells you something. After all, you need to have faith in something, right? When God spoke to Abraham, we are told that Abraham believed God. He put faith in the words God spoke, believing God would fulfill them. This whole process of having faith God can test assumes we believe God when he tells us something, just as Abraham did.

Second, persecution arises because of the word God spoke to you. Jesus makes this clear when He explains the parable of the sower. He says the seed is the "word of the kingdom" (Matthew 13:19). More than just the gospel of salvation, this word of the kingdom is anything God speaks to us intending to grow his kingdom in us, which is basically any time he speaks to us. Then Jesus drops the bomb—persecution arises *because of* the word God spoke to us (v. 21). This is when it looks like hope is gone and God's word won't come to pass. You don't see the happy ending.

Now there's a small but important clarification I need to insert here, because a lot of people say every difficulty they face is a trial from God. They think anything difficult—from an overbearing boss to cancer to the loss of a child—is a storm sent on their life by God to refine their character. There are two problems with this belief, and they both have to do with not realizing that God's trials are trials of faith. First, a trial of faith will be specific, directly opposing the word God spoke to us. It's not general hardship and suffering. Second, it's a trial of faith, not of character. God's intended fruit is endurance, leading to our being perfect and complete, lacking in nothing. Clearly, these are ingredients to victorious, powerful living, not suffering, oppressed living—no matter how righteous that oppressed life is.

Some difficulties we face are because we have a living but defeated enemy who hates us. This is an attack we overcome by clinging to and declaring the victory Jesus won for us and standing firm in who he says we are. Some difficulties we face are because we sowed bad choices and reap painful consequences. This is the school of hard knocks, not the judgment or discipline of God, and the good news is we can graduate by learning wisdom and not repeating mistakes. Either way, it's not a trial of faith and we shouldn't treat it like one. If we do treat it like a trial of faith, we can empower either the enemy or our own stupidity to continue wreaking destruction in our lives.

Third, in a genuine trial of faith, you face a choice: endure or move on. If you choose to hold fast in faith, to say, "I know what God said and I will remain in him!" it will produce steadfastness, or endurance. The strategy to do this, almost every time, is to change what we believe—not to white-knuckle our way through the situation.

In the parable of the sower, persecution rises against the word only when it falls on rocky ground and is received with joy but finds no place for deep roots. The rocks in this ground are symbolic of strongholds like Paul references in 2 Corinthians 10:4-5—patterns of thought that war against the knowledge of God. The only solution for these strongholds in our own belief system is to renew our mind until it conforms to God's truth.

In other words, God will often aim his words to us directly at the mindsets we have that are keeping us from becoming who he made us to be. He introduces conflict into our lives to highlight those areas to us so we are no longer ignorant about those things that hold us back. This is part of his process of discipline (revisit chapter 8 to see more on this process).

Fourth, the endurance we choose has a perfect result, making us perfect and complete, lacking in nothing. Read that again and let it sink in, because those are some pretty amazing words God would use to describe you and me.

Not coincidentally, the next verse says, "If any of you lacks wisdom, let him ask God, who gives to all generously and without reproach, and it will be given him" (James 1:5). Wisdom is defined as knowing what to do. If you're in the middle of a trial, that's exactly what you need. Mercifully, there's never shame in needing, asking for, or receiving wisdom.

However, we should pay attention to an important distinction. Our request for wisdom most often isn't "God, should I stay here?" Usually, it's a "God, this is a tough situation. What am I supposed to do?" We approach this by viewing ourselves as overcomers who are capable and powerful to bring change to hopeless situations.

This is God's process of promise. He promises something to us. That promise forces us to wrestle with our faith, whether we really believe God. As we stubbornly let the wrestling change our minds about how good God is and who he says we are—by delighting in the Lord—we become changed into his likeness. By being changed into his likeness, we become perfect and complete, lacking in nothing. And through it all, we develop the right mindsets we need to support the promise he gave us when it is fulfilled.

VISION BRINGS FOCUS

Now you know what's going on when all that craziness happens after God makes a promise to you or gives you a word, and you know at least one major reason why he says we should befriend faithfulness and wait for the fulfillment of our desires. Knowing these things is huge. Oftentimes, just knowing what's going on is enough to keep us from going crazy when life is hard.

But I'm going to give you another tool as well, one that is incredibly powerful for getting us through the times when it feels like God's promises will just never come to pass. This tool is vision.

Vision is simply knowing clearly where you are going in life. I've seen many Christians intentionally forsake vision because they believe God should be in charge of their lives. And it's not that he shouldn't. We should listen to him and follow his words, but he will teach us to have a vision for our lives. We can't embrace fatalism and call it God's will. For God's will to be done, we have to become active participants.

What about God being sovereign? Yes, he is sovereign, but Scripture still tells us that his will is that none should perish (2 Peter 3:9), yet we know many will. So obviously there are times when God's will is not fulfilled, and it's because he's given us authority to choose. This means we need to take responsibility for our own lives, first to hear from God about who he made us to be and the promises he has for us, and second to own that vision and the responsibility for walking it out in relationship with God.

Paul reveals something very interesting about God's will when he tells us that one of the fruits of the Spirit is self-control. I thought for years that God wanted to control my life, so I kept trying to give that control to him. Eventually I realized that self-control really does mean that; it does not mean God-control. God's desire is to set us free from every work of the devil that would try to control us. It's Satan who wants to control us through fear, manipulation, deceit, sickness, and sin, but God wants us to be free. That's why a fruit of his work in our lives is the freedom of self-control.

I've never known any genuine Christian who didn't want to please God. If they struggled to do this, it often became nearly torturous to them that they failed to do what they wanted to do. They weren't free. The issue was they didn't have self-control, because if they had control of themselves, they wouldn't have chosen sin. Their problem wasn't a lack of submission to God; it was a lack of freedom from Satan's tools of control. Once we gain freedom from the works of the devil, we have the self-control to follow God with our freedom. This is what God wants for our lives, and he inspires us toward this goal with his promises of the great future he has for us.

God wants us to be led by a vision for our lives. What does vision do for us? It keeps us focused. Proverbs 29:18 tells us, "Where there is no prophetic vision the people cast off restraint." In other words, when you don't know what God says about your life, it's easy to wander aimlessly, not knowing where you're going. But when you have a word from God about who you are and why he created you, it gives you vision and purpose to restrain your choices and keep you on track.

There is a reason why every successful business has clearly articulated their vision. They know why they exist and what they aim to accomplish. If you've ever been in business for yourself, you understand this has to be a lot more specific than, "We want to make lots of money by selling lots of product." Sure, you want to sell tons of your products or services so you can make money, but what products? What services? Who are you going to sell to? And ultimately, here's the big question: why are you going to do what you do?

If what you do doesn't strike gold somewhere deep inside you that this is what you were created to do, it won't hold you for very long. Certainly, it won't hold you through the difficult times that try to knock you off course. But when you know that you know that you know that you know this is absolutely who you are and that's going to be who you are no matter what position you hold, you can remain steady until the promise comes to pass.

VALUES GUIDE DECISIONS

Something I said there right at the end is a lot bigger than it sounded: being yourself regardless of the position you hold. There's a truth in the kingdom of God that you will need to serve before God will promote you. Jesus directly says, "If you have not been faithful in that which is another's, who will give you that which is your own?" (Luke 16:12). This is a principle he uses as he runs his kingdom, which guarantees we will learn through service.

So let's say God tells you he is making you his prophet to the nations. He is going to send you before royalty and business leaders and you will minister to millions of people. Or let's say he's going to give you business ideas that revolutionize a particular industry and will make you billions of dollars. Or let's say he's going to anoint you as a performer and you are going to bring his kingdom like never before to Hollywood or Broadway. Whatever the word is, it's amazing. This principle means you're going to learn your craft in a place that's likely to be hidden and obscure while serving someone else with no promise they are going to be pleasant to serve.

As disagreeable as that sounds, I wouldn't spare anyone even the smallest fragment of this part of the process because promoting someone before they learn to serve only works to destroy both them and anything they are given authority over. It ruins the promise and the person, so it's very important. But I want to get to my point, which isn't about serving; it's about how to live authentically regardless of your position. It's the key to both serving well and being promoted well.

If vision helps sustain you through the process, your values will tell you how to live both during the process and beyond. They are what you hold most dear, the things that go beyond what is just important to you to what is truly critical to you in life. Because they are so important to you, your values guide your decisions so that you always make room for them.

My family has worked to develop our core values. I teach my children, even from their young ages, that "to be a White means we are loving, wise, generational, earnest, thankful, children of God." For us, this means we are:

- Loving: This is how we behave toward ourselves, one another, and those outside our family. It restrains our words and actions to those that communicate honor and significance.

- Wise: This means we face every problem with confidence, knowing we possess the creativity needed to address it successfully. It also determines the way we manage ourselves financially, relationally, and in all our responsibilities.

- Generational: This means our lives are not for or from ourselves, but we are anchored in a heritage that began long before us and we live to provide a rich legacy to the generations that come after us. We honor past generations to learn from their failures and build on their successes while promoting our children in a way that celebrates when they surpass us.

- Earnest: This means we are completely honest and authentic, both in our identity and in the work we do. We live true to the identity God gives us, and we work faithfully with integrity to steward those things he has placed under our authority.

- Thankful: This means we keep perspective regarding where our lives and blessings come from, never forgetting our God who makes every good thing possible. It also determines our attitude in every relationship, remaining thankful for each person because of who God made them to be.

- Children of God: This is the value that establishes our relationship with God. All our other values are empty without this taking precedence over all.

Every major decision we make as a family has to run through these filters. If it doesn't fit who we are as Whites, we don't do it.

Conversely, we can proactively dream of things to do that very much fit our values and pursue them wholeheartedly. We know these values agree with God's Word, so anything we do from these values is going to be something God approves. These values give us freedom to dream, the ability to live confidently, and a healthy accountability that will keep us on the path toward our vision.

DISCOVER YOUR VISION AND VALUES

Developing your vision and values can take time, and it starts by inviting God to speak to you about who you are. There are, however, some very simple tools that can help bring clarity to them quickly.

First, use the five whys tool. Start with something that's important to you. Just name anything—cleanliness, punctuality, fun, impact, family, godliness, etc.—and ask yourself (or have someone else ask you) why it is important to you. Then ask why that is important to you. Then ask why that is important to you. Ask this same question—why—five times. Generally speaking, by the time you have rooted down that deep into why something is important to you, you have gotten past the surface things to the core of what really drives your decisions.

A friend of mine started this exercise by saying cleanliness was important to her. By the second and third whys, she started to realize that having time and space for family was actually the reason cleanliness was important to her. Having things clean wasn't important to her in and of itself, but only because it set the stage for impactful interactions with family. She was astonished that her value for such mundane tasks (and she is very much a task-oriented person) was actually relationships. This helped her manage chores in her house very differently, not driving to get her children to help her accomplish something, but bringing them in as helpers to facilitate relationship in their home. It made a big difference!

Second, make a list of your top one hundred dreams for your life. It doesn't matter what these dreams are, just write them down. I find it helpful to work in veins—travel, learning (new degrees, languages, instruments, etc.), family, occupation, spiritual life, experiences (sky diving, sporting events, concerts, etc.), and more. Some of these dreams will seem frivolous, but write them down anyway.

After you complete your list, let it sit for a week or two and then narrow it down to your top fifty. Don't let yourself just write fifty and assume it's your top fifty. Take the time to dig deep enough to come up with a hundred, then narrow it down. You'll get a truer sense of what's most important to you.

Finally, narrow your list to twenty-five. Look for themes and commonalities; these will give you clues into what your most deeply held values are and where you want your life to go.

Third, write your own obituary. I know this seems morbid, but the heart of this is to articulate how you want to be remembered. These are the things you want people to say about you after you die, the headlines of your life.

Complete all three of these activities and you will have a great start on discovering your core values. Then talk to God about what you've discovered. Ask him what he thinks about your results. If you're willing to hear him truly, he'll breathe life into your dreams and cheer you on to incredible things you never really believed were possible.

Another friend of mine once did this dreams exercise in an identity class I was teaching. She wrestled with God over one particular dream that was so far gone to her that she considered it dead, buried, and with grass on the grave and a tree that had grown up beside it. It was so dead that "dead" barely says how dead it was. She truly thought that dream could never happen, and she refused to talk to anyone about it. Even thinking about it was painful, and writing it down as a dream was worse because then she had to hope for it again. But she knew God was telling her to do it, so she did. About a year after she wrote the dream down, she got to see God fulfill it. You never know what God will do if you just write the dream down and invite him into the process.

Last of all, look over all those dreams and the core values you've discovered. Read the obituary you wrote for yourself. Then ask yourself, *If these things are so important to me that I want them to outlive me, why don't I begin living for them right now?*

This is the life God has created you for. What are you waiting for? Dream with God, then start living toward that dream today.

SECTION THREE:
BE FREE

Chapter 12

CREATED TO RULE

The image of God is who we were created to be, but what were we created to do? God's original declaration over humankind unleashed a powerful statement about our purpose. Giving us room to dream with God about the life we can have in him, this statement is strong, free, important, and good. It is God's declaration that we were created to rule!

One day I sat with my dad, talking over my decision about which colleges I should apply to and what major I should choose. He could tell I was more stressed over these decisions than I should be. This became one of those times where the significance of the moment immediately outgrew its context as my dad said something to me that I still often tell myself today.

My dad said to me, "Nathanael, it's like you're at the base of one mountain, but you're trying to see to the opposite base of two mountains away. You just can't see that far. You're going to have to make the decisions in front of you now and then just keep figuring things out as you go."

I needed those words. I needed them because I have always tried to live twenty years in the future. As I sat there with my dad that day, my plan was to serve God on the mission field for the rest of my life after college. I felt that I needed to know what mission organization I would be with, what kind of missions I would be doing, and what country I would live in before I could choose which college and major would best prepare me for the life that came after college. I desperately wanted to understand my purpose—what I would be doing—so I could be prepared to do a good job when the right time came.

As it turns out, I never could have imagined the road God would lead me down in the years following that conversation. While I wanted to understand my purpose, God wanted me to first understand who I am. He certainly has great purposes for me, but he always wanted those purposes to be anchored in the identity he created for me. It has been in discovering that identity over the past fourteen years that I have also discovered my purpose.

BEING BECOMES DOING

At the opening of this book, we started with the classic questions *Why am I here?* and *Why was I born?* We saw how God answered these right from the very beginning, that the answer we had searched to find for so long had been hidden right out in the open when God declared, "Let us make man in our image, after our likeness" (Genesis 1:26).

This statement establishes our identity, but there are two sides to our existence. The side we have talked about up to this point is all about who we are—it is our "being." But every "being" has to go somewhere. It can't just sit there by itself or it won't come to its ultimate fulfillment and joy. We can't be content with just "being"; we have to find our "doing" as well.

We have to find the "doing" that goes with our "being" because we are made in the image of God. One of the most special revelations God gives us about himself comes from the name by which he made himself known to Moses. When Moses encountered God in the burning bush, he asked God his name so he could tell the Israelites who had sent him to them.

God said, "I Am. Tell them I Am has sent you to them" (my paraphrase). What's most incredible to me about this name is that it's one of

CREATED TO RULE

the only names in Scripture God uses for himself. There are literally dozens of other names people call God in Scripture, and almost all of them have the "I Am" at the core of them. You have Jehovah Jireh—I Am who Provides. You have Jehovah Shalom—I Am Peace. And you have many, many others like this.

Each of these names of God reveals something he does (his "doing") because of who he is (his "being"). If it wasn't part of his identity, it wouldn't be part of his actions toward us. He does out of who he is. Every purpose of his deeds is rooted in the identity of his being. He doesn't just do something because it needs to be done; he does it because it's an outflow of who he is.

So when he provides for someone, he does it because provision and generosity are part of his nature. It might help us understand this better to look at a contrast. If you compared God's provision with Satan's provision, you see even more clearly how God's provision is a revelation of his nature. The only reason Satan would care to provide for someone is the same as the only reason a drug dealer gives free samples—to manipulate, ensnare, trap, and control. But God's provision comes with no strings attached. It comes from his generous goodness. His actions aren't done in isolation, but instead come from his character—his "doing" comes from his "being."

We are created the same way. Our existence begins with who we are, but if who we are never extends to our actions, then it's empty and meaningless. Our "being" has to turn into "doing."

This leads all of us to some new questions. After we answer the question of who we are created to be—that unique manifestation of God's image that no one else could ever become—we have to ask two questions: *What was I created to do?* and *What is my purpose?*

GOD DECLARES OUR PURPOSE

In the very beginning, God declared our identity first. Our "being" always comes before our "doing." Who we are always takes precedent over what we do. But immediately after God declared who we are, he also declared our purpose. He said, "Let us make man in our image, after our likeness. *And let them have dominion*" (Genesis 1:26).

We learn more about what he meant just a couple verses later, where we read:

> And God blessed them. And God said to them, "Be fruitful and multiply and fill the earth and subdue it, and have dominion over the fish of the sea and over the birds of the heavens and over every living thing that moves on the earth."—v. 28

There's a lot of depth in this verse that is well worth going into, but we're only going to take a cursory look into it here. What God says is that he gave authority over the earth to humankind. It was completely up to us to take charge of earth and make it into all it could be.

When you look at the description of the world in the beginning, you see that there was a garden in a land called Eden in the eastern region of the world. The assignment God gave Adam and Eve was to cultivate and keep this garden until it covered the world. The perfect realities of the garden were to become the perfect realities of the entire world.

We already took a long look at what happened instead when Adam chose independence over relationship, plunging humankind into sin and shame and relegating us to relate to God through rules that defined good and evil. But there's at least one more important thing to say about the rules God eventually gave Israel—in revealing what God is like, they also secretly taught Israel how to be like God. During the short periods of time when Israel followed God's laws, they became more conformed to his image, and, through that, they more closely fulfilled the reason God made them.

We can see throughout Israel's history that whenever Israel lived more closely to God's image, God also gave them dominion over their land. But whenever they disobeyed his rules, distancing themselves from his image, he also took away dominion from them by allowing their enemies to encroach on their cities, overpower them, and enslave them.

Likeness and dominion are inseparable themes throughout Scripture. They always go hand in hand. As likeness increases, so does dominion, and it's no wonder, because God created us for both of them from the very beginning.

THE GOSPEL OF THE KINGDOM

It makes sense then that just as Jesus came to restore our relationship with God and make it possible for us to fulfill his intent in creating us, he also came preaching the good news of his kingdom.

At its very heart, a kingdom is a king's dominion, the territory where he rules and reigns. And from the very beginning of Jesus' ministry, we see that the coming of God's kingdom was the core of his message. The beginning of Jesus' ministry happened like this: Jesus was baptized, then led into the wilderness by the Holy Spirit, and when he came out, he began his ministry in power. But Matthew records the first part of Jesus' ministry by saying, "From that time Jesus began to preach, saying, 'Repent, for the kingdom of heaven is at hand'" (Matthew 4:17).

There are three things we need to see here. First, we see that this was Jesus' primary message throughout his life. We know that because Matthew says, "From that time Jesus began to preach." That means this was the heart of Jesus' message everywhere he went.

Second, we see Jesus calling people to repent. The Greek word for repent is *metanoeō*, and it literally means "to change one's mind."[11] We have come to use "repent" as a word calling people to change the way they live, or to confess they have been living as they shouldn't. Maybe this is an accurate way to use it, but it's not the way Jesus used it. We know this because Jesus told us specifically what he wants us to change our minds about.

This is the third thing we see here. The call Jesus made to the people was for them to realize that the kingdom of heaven is at hand. This was and still is revolutionary, because for something to be at hand means it is within reach. When I am at work, I like to have my coffee at hand so I can reach out, grab my mug, and take a sip (or even a swig).

All the Jews who heard Jesus' message expected an earthly messiah who would establish an earthly kingdom to dominate all other kingdoms, but Jesus came with the message that God's heavenly kingdom was within reach for every one of them. He then demonstrated his message with power by making heaven's realities manifest on earth, healing all who were sick, casting out demons everywhere he went, setting captives free, and making the infirm whole. Jesus made right all those earthly maladies you would never find in heaven, declaring to everyone who saw the signs that heaven was within reach if they would only change their minds to believe it.

When Jesus brought the message of the kingdom, he took our created purpose of having dominion to a whole new level, because while this message of the kingdom was Jesus' life message, it was not only his life message. It was also the message into which he discipled the disciples. Matthew 10 records the story of when Jesus sent out his twelve disciples into various cities, instructing them, "Proclaim as you go, saying, 'The kingdom of heaven is at hand.' Heal the sick, raise the dead, cleanse lepers, cast out demons" (vv. 10:8). Jesus sent his disciples with the same message he preached and the same ministry he did.

More than that, Jesus' training of others into this message and ministry went even beyond the disciples. Luke 10 tells us about when Jesus sent seventy-two people out into the cities where he was about to go. He instructed them, "Whenever you enter a town and they receive you, eat what is set before you. Heal the sick in it and say to them, 'The kingdom of God has come near to you'" (Luke 10:8–9).

Jesus' message of the kingdom was never just his message; it was the message he imparted to everyone who followed him. In all, the word *kingdom* is used 158 times in the New Testament, and 131 of those are specifically tied to being either the kingdom of heaven or the kingdom of God (which are the same thing).[12] For comparison, the word *love* is used 179 times,[13] the word *grace* is used 131 times,[14] and the word *salvation* is used only 45 times.[15] All this shows us that the theme of the kingdom of heaven is just as major a theme in the New Testament as love and grace, and in some ways is even more emphasized than salvation.

I'll toss one more Scripture from Jesus' time on earth at you and then we'll look at what it all means for us. After Jesus rose from the dead, he had forty days to spend with his disciples and pass on to them anything he wanted. He could have talked to them about the Holy Spirit. He could have told them about the transitions they were about to go through. He could have taught them about anything at all, but Acts 1:3 tells us that every conversation he had with them shared one common theme. I'm sure by now you can guess what it was. Acts 1:3 says, "[Jesus] presented himself alive to them after his suffering by many proofs, appearing to them during forty days and *speaking about the kingdom of God.*"

Of all the things Jesus could have taught them, he chose one thing—the kingdom. To help articulate just how mind-blowing this is to me, I need to expose a little more of my geek side that revisits the time when I was choosing a college.

When I visited the school I would eventually attend, I pored over their student handbook and read the required class lists for various majors. Every degree the school offered included four major theology classes and a smattering of classes that focused on various books of the Bible. There were extra theology electives students could take as well. I remember one that particularly stood out to me—the Theology of Suffering.

All of those classes were and are important, but as I look back on that experience, I can't remember one class that specifically focused on the kingdom. After twenty years of being deeply involved in church, I didn't even know there should be a class on the kingdom. Yet from looking at Jesus' life and ministry, maybe every class should have been focused on the kingdom, because that was the focus of every message Jesus ever preached or taught others to preach.

DISCIPLING NATIONS

Because the message of the kingdom was so central to Jesus' ministry, we could go on forever looking at passages to show just how central this message was, but you get the point. What we need to know now is what this means to us today. To uncover that, we are going to look at these verses:

> And Jesus came and said to them, "All authority in heaven and on earth has been given to me. Go therefore and make disciples of all nations, baptizing them in the name of the Father and of the Son and of the Holy Spirit, teaching them to observe all that I have commanded you. And behold, I am with you always, to the end of the age."—Matthew 28:18–20

This is a well-known passage often referred to as the Great Commission. It was Jesus' final words to his followers before returning to heaven as recorded by Matthew. He begins with an interesting statement, if you wonder at all why he would tell them all authority had been given to him. Why would that matter? Especially why would it matter to him saying, "Go *therefore* and make disciples of all nations"? What did Jesus' authority have to do with his command for us to go?

I'll leave you with that question for a moment while we look at an often-overlooked part of what Jesus says next—to go make disciples of all nations. Make sure you read that carefully, because most people read what they assume Jesus meant instead of what he actually said, and I was guilty of this for years until someone pointed it out to me. Jesus did not say make disciples *in* all nations; he said make disciples *of* all nations.

That one little word makes a *big* difference! We are not called to only make individual disciples here and there throughout the world, but to also radically change the way nations throughout the world operate. To do that, every realm of society has to change. Government, business, entertainment, family, media, the economy, and every other stratus of society has to become influenced by God's kingdom, being discipled into all Jesus commanded.

And what was that, exactly? What did Jesus command? What message had he discipled his disciples into? It was the message of the kingdom! It was the good news that dominion has been restored to humankind.

What Adam and Eve had lost in the garden—likeness to God and the ability to extend God's perfect realities throughout earth—Jesus restored. He brought us back into relationship with God so that through the Holy Spirit we can be made like him again. Then all authority in heaven and on earth was given to him so he could send us with a New Testament version of what God had once upon a time said to Adam and Eve: "Be fruitful and multiply and fill the earth and subdue it" (Genesis 1:28).

Jesus' command is the perfect mirror to that original command. Our first father and mother were to fill the earth, and we are to do the same, obeying the command to go. Adam and Eve were commanded to subdue the earth, and we are to do the same by making disciples of all nations, teaching the nations of the earth to submit themselves to God's rule.

Lest anyone misunderstand what I mean by this, don't forget the context of this entire book and take what I just said to mean something it doesn't. God doesn't rule the way the world does. He does it the opposite way. Remember that Jesus didn't come serve on earth for thirty-three years, pretending to be a servant so he could retire to a pension in heaven where everything could be all about him again. No, he has always been a servant and always will be a servant.

Discipling nations into all Jesus commanded us means we teach nations to love, to serve, and to exalt its people the same way God loves, serves, and exalts us. It doesn't in any way—and could not ever, possibly, even remotely, in any way—resemble a military-like domination and subjugation of one nation over another to force them to follow rules that relegate people to becoming cheap imitations of God instead of supernaturally transformed images of God. Jesus had plenty of opportunities to become that kind of messiah, and he rejected all of them. He chose instead to become a messiah who ushered in a kingdom that is birthed from heaven into earth through those who are being inwardly transformed into his image so their outward influence really does become heavenly.

LIVE YOUR PURPOSE

This is God's purpose for your life: anything that builds his kingdom. Ready, go.

It's that simple. If you look at Adam and Eve, with what God instructed them in the beginning, he didn't tell them how to accomplish their commission. They could be fruitful and multiply, filling the earth and subduing it any way they found worked. They had freedom, and so do you. You have freedom to become who God made you to be, to walk in the unique identity God made for you and is creating you into. Through that identity, you have the ability to be creative, to dream, and to pursue any and every opportunity you can find to release the heavenly realities you have discovered to the world around you.

Like Jesus and his disciples, this can look like healing the sick, cleansing the lepers, casting out demons, and raising the dead. Because all authority is his and he has sent you, all authority is now also in your hands. And because he has given his Holy Spirit to you, you have the ability to look at the earthly circumstances around you, imagine how they would change if they were transported to heaven, and then release the transformation heaven would bring to earth.

It can look like being a friend to friendless people, housing the homeless, visiting the sick and imprisoned, and caring for orphans. This is the kingdom.

It can look like starting businesses that serve God before money, not rejecting success and prosperity (Solomon certainly didn't) but using them to even further disciple nations. When I traveled once to Togo, I met a man who was simply an accountant. This is already a highly educated position for anyone to have in that country, but as we met him and began to prophesy over him, God spoke to us about how he would have opportunities to work with the highest levels of government in his country to help them remove the corruption that keeps their economy from growing. We declared over him that God would give him wisdom to disciple his nation into the kingdom to such an extent that other African nations would come to them to learn how to overcome corruption. That is the kingdom!

Another businessman we met on that trip is forging a new industry in his nation, working to bring sustainable organic chicken farming to Togo. He is a man of integrity, doing things the right way against the grain of a system that rewards people who are willing to use bribes and shortcuts. We prophesied hope over him, telling him that his work and example has great influence in the business community of his nation. This is the kingdom too.

Your opportunities are truly endless. God's image must be carried to every realm of society so that those who don't know they were born to carry his image can awaken to this truth, become transformed into their unique image, and begin taking that image and the influence that goes with it into their homes and communities.

WHAT ABOUT YOUR CALLING?

There's one huge question many people will still have after all I've said so far, and it has to do with discovering your calling. The calling on someone's life has been the main topic of somewhat regular conversations in my life for the past ten to fifteen years. I've had these conversations in living rooms, dorm rooms, coffee shops, hotel conference rooms, church sanctuaries, and probably just about everywhere else too.

Because this has been such a huge issue over so many years, I finally studied the issue of callings in Scripture. I looked up every passage that used the word *calling* to see how it is used throughout the Bible. What I can tell you is that there is a definite universal meaning God has when he talks about our calling. When he talks about our calling, he is speaking about our salvation. There is literally no exception to this in Scripture.

What does that mean for you and me? It means God calls us to become saved. Does it mean he has no further plan for our lives beyond that? No, of course he has plans and purposes beyond that, but it's not like

God has one specific plan for us and if we somehow miss that one plan then we've messed everything up.

You can't destroy God's "call" on your life. You can't undo his plan or purpose for you, because he doesn't have just one. One of the passages on calling helps make this clear:

> To this end we always pray for you, *that our God may make you worthy of his calling and may fulfill every resolve for good and every work of faith by his power*, so that the name of our Lord Jesus may be glorified in you, and you in him, according to the grace of our God and the Lord Jesus Christ.—2 Thessalonians 1:11–12

Paul writes here to the church of the city Thessalonica, a group of people, about the calling they all share in common—the calling to salvation—telling them he prays that God would make them worthy of their salvation. That's a bit heavy, right there, if you ask me. "I pray that God would make you worth the price he paid for you, that Jesus' death on your behalf wouldn't have been a waste." That's scary to think about, so I pray each of us lives a life that proves us worth the cost of our salvation, the cost of the calling we all share together.

This common calling is not an individual call placed upon anyone's life addressed in this letter. Instead, Paul continues in his prayer that God would "fulfill every resolve for good and every work of faith by his power." Now that makes our Christian life pretty simple. We are called to salvation; live to prove you're worth the cost Jesus paid. Do that by resolving to do some good in this world. What good? Who cares? Just resolve to do some good! Choose something! Then ask God to help you, so that he may fulfill your resolve for good by his power.

Oh, and when you resolve to do something good, choose something big enough that you can't do it alone. Choose something that requires God's involvement, something that requires you to need faith for it. Be daring. Take a risk in what you resolve to do. If we will do this, it will both glorify the name of Jesus in us and us in him.

CREATED TO RULE

What you might perceive as your "calling," according to how people use that word today, is really your identity. It is what is unique to you alone that only you can become—but it is who you become, not what you do, that is unique. God has an identity reserved just for you, and you can't miss it; you'll become it more and more your entire life as long as you are pursuing Jesus Christ with all your heart, soul, mind, and strength.

As you become you, resolve to do some good with yourself. The beauty of this is that there are no rules placed on you. The only boundary is your identity. Don't try to build God's kingdom in a way you weren't created to. If you dream of businesses, don't try to pastor a church. If you dream of acting, don't go into business. If God's presence drops on the room every time you sing, maybe you should find a way to do that.

But I can't tell you what to do. Someone might have a prophetic word that confirms what's already in your heart, but only God can tell you who you are, and he is the one who will best know where your identity will be most fulfilled as you work out your purpose of building his kingdom somewhere in this world.

I should also note that one identity might seem like a dream to one person, but a nightmare to another. Someone may know deep in their heart they are created for public platforms, while someone else shudders at that idea and thrives in hidden roles. All roles are important, and even necessary. Never feel ashamed of your role. The most hidden and overlooked role is just as important, powerful, and impactful as the most visible and celebrated—as long as it is who God created you to be.

I will also say that almost always God will give those in authority over your life insight into your life, so they are often great people to ask for input regarding where specifically your identity and purpose meet together. And I will also say that only fools isolate themselves away from the input of others who can point out blind spots or encourage us through the humble beginnings. So don't go alone. Go with community and go with counsel. But please go. Go be who God created you to be. Start by discovering your "being." But then let that guide you to your purpose within his kingdom. Accomplish your "doing."

Only when you put your "being" and your "doing" together will you have life as God intended it to be. After all, that is what he declared at the very beginning.

Chapter 13

GOD FOLLOWS YOU

When we first believe in Jesus, we have to follow him for a time to learn how to live as he does. His process teaches us his heart, and once we know his heart, he begins to empower us to make our own decisions. His goal is not that we would follow him our entire life, but that we would grow to a point where he begins to follow us.

God must have been smiling as he took me through a deep process, knowing the depth of it would mark me indelibly for the rest of my life. Or maybe he just knew I was strong-willed and needed such a deep process for it to actually stick. Either way, I can still remember the pain of that season as I longed for more of God but he felt just out of reach.

That season began when I started journaling for the first time in my life. It was just an inch of page space each night, but it got me started. The act of journaling became God's opportunity to speak to me about my life, and about patterns of behavior that became easier to see when I started keeping track. It was clear I wasn't as good of a Christian as I had maybe thought.

It all worked together to stir something in the deepest place inside me, and really, it was his Spirit moving in me. Very quickly, I knew God was placing a demand on me—he wanted my life, and he wanted it all.

I said it was a painful season, but the pain was one of lack and longing. Though it happened so long ago, I still struggle to put words to what it was like. The best I have come up with is to say that it was like God would draw near enough to allow me to feel how amazing he is, but not close enough for me to really embrace him. Though Jesus lived in my heart, he was not in charge of it, and because of that I knew I lacked the fullness of what he offered me. The lack felt like a vacuum inside me that would never be satisfied until I committed my all to God and received all of him in return.

Really, God was offering as much of himself to me as I was offering of myself to him. I wanted all of him without giving all of myself, and he drew a healthy boundary that kept me from abusing my relationship with him. But he stayed close enough to me that I knew if I would give my all, I would receive his all in return. Eventually, my whole heart got behind the words I had tried to confess many times, and in one powerful moment I abandoned the throne of my life to Jesus.

So began the season of my life in which I followed Jesus. There was no question who was in charge; Jesus was. It was a refining season many years long. I remember my relationship with Jesus during those years as being filled with corrections, not inspirations. Much of it was learning overtly how *not* to live and more subtly learning how *to* live.

I have to say, however, that those correction-filled years were my problem. I didn't know how to hear his voice clearly. I knew his Word, and I knew I was stuck in things he said were wrong, which made me assume he was always correcting me. As I look back on it, the moments when I know for sure I heard his voice, he only ever spoke to me about the way of life and the actions that would lead to his best.

Eventually, someone taught me how to become confident in hearing God's voice (thank you, Jamey VanGelder!). God started talking to me about who I am. He cast vision for my life. He strengthened me with confidence and healed me of wounds and lies that bound me to insecurities and fears. He taught me healthy values and mindsets to shape my decisions so I could finally choose wisely.

EXTRAORDINARY CIRCUMSTANCES

That's when God surprised me one day as I read the story of Joshua, showing me a powerful truth hidden in a verse many people know well. I'll give you all the verses we'll look at, but we'll spend most of our time in the final verse:

> *"Be strong and courageous*, for you shall cause this people to inherit the land that I swore to their fathers to give them. *Only be strong and very courageous*, being careful to do according to all the law that Moses my servant commanded you. Do not turn from it to the right hand or to the left, that you may have good success wherever you go. This Book of the Law shall not depart from your mouth, but you shall meditate on it day and night, so that you may be careful to do according to all that is written in it. For then you will make your way prosperous, and then you will have good success. Have I not commanded you? *Be strong and courageous. Do not be frightened, and do not be dismayed, for the* LORD *your God is with you wherever you go."*—Joshua 1:6–9

You might have noticed, but God really must have wanted to encourage Joshua to be brave. He actually tells him to be strong and courageous three separate times, throwing the word *very* in there once for good measure.

Joshua had good reason to need this sort of encouragement. God had just told him Moses was dead, which meant Joshua was now officially the sole leader of two million people. He knew it was coming, but you might imagine how different it would be when suddenly you are no longer an assistant to the big man and have become the big man yourself.

This is a huge change, but it was the smallest change Joshua had to navigate at that time. Much more significantly, as soon as the Israelites passed into the Promised Land, the manna they had relied on for forty years stopped coming. They crossed the Jordan River, ate the food of the land, and that was the last day they ever had manna. Their supernatural provision, which by that time would have felt like an incredible security blanket, was gone. Most of the army Joshua took with him had never known life without manna every day, but as soon as Joshua took over the manna disappeared. Yikes! But don't be afraid, Joshua; don't be afraid. With no manna to tell him that God was still with him, he probably needed this reassuring promise.

But hold on, because as rough as losing Moses and the manna would have been, a third loss would have been the worst of all. Every day since the day they set out from Egypt, God had led the people with a pillar of fire by night and cloud by day. Once in the Promised Land, God no longer led them this way. The pillar went away. The people, who had lived most or all of their lives able to see God's manifest presence visibly among them in the center of their camp, could no longer see him. For the first time in their life, they actually needed to have faith that God was with them. Again, this just so happened to correspond to Joshua taking over leadership of the nation.

Could you imagine the headlines if something similar happened when one president of the United States took over for another? What if one had God visibly with him, giving the entire nation supernatural provision every day, but as soon as the next leader took over, both the provision and the vision of God disappeared? I'm sure the majority of the nation would be calling for his head. Polls would go out, asking what should be done with the new leader. Should we stop at simply deposing him, or should we go all the way and execute him for the heathen he obviously must be for God to abandon him like that?

I can't imagine what it would be like to take over leadership of two million people under any circumstances, let alone those circumstances. That was really a time when Joshua needed a promise that God would never leave him or forsake him, but would surely be with him wherever he went.

WHO FOLLOWS WHOM?

Let's take another look at what God said to Joshua at the end there, within the context of how Joshua had related to God for the previous forty years.

As I said, ever since Joshua left Egypt, God had led Israel wherever they went with a pillar of cloud or fire. God's visible presence was an ever-present reality.

But there's an important detail about how this pillar–nation relationship worked. God, in the pillar, completely directed ever major move the camp of Israel made. When the pillar rose up, the people packed up. When the pillar moved, the people moved. When the pillar stopped, the people stopped. And however long the pillar remained, the people would also remain. Israel literally followed God as he led them stage by stage through the wilderness.

After forty years, there would be a comfort in knowing someone else was in charge of directions. It would be easy to check out mentally, not paying much attention, because the only responsibility anyone had was to follow. I recently watched *Good Will Hunting*, a movie made only twenty years ago, and had to smile when one character said to another that they would be traveling but there would be an answering machine they would check from time to time.[16]

This is the technology I grew up with, so I understood it completely, but if my children ever watch that movie, they might not get that line at all. In just twenty years, that is how used to cell phones I, and we as a culture, have become—and I've only had one for about twelve years. Now imagine how used to something you would be if you had it for forty years, especially if those forty years were your entire life. This is how normal life with the visible presence of God was for Israel. It's how unspectacular God's leadership through the wilderness and the daily manna could have become to them. God led them, God fed them; this was life for all of Israel, including Joshua—until now.

I'm telling you this was a really big deal! God's presence disappeared! His leader on earth was dead! His gift of daily food stopped coming! This is the breach into which Joshua was thrust, tasked with not only managing this incredibly transition but also conquering a land filled with nations stronger and more numerous than his own. In that context, mark God's specific words: "Be strong and courageous. Do not be frightened, and do not be dismayed, *for the* LORD *your God is with you wherever you go*" (Joshua 1:9). Did you catch that? For forty years, Joshua had been with God wherever God went, but now God said he would be with Joshua wherever Joshua went.

Whoa. That is the most major transition of any we have yet talked about here, bigger than Moses to Joshua, manna to harvested crops, or visible presence to invisible presence. This is a transition from man following God to God following man.

JOSHUA PASSED HIS SCHOOLING

Did you hear me? God said he would follow Joshua! If you're like me when I first realized this truth, you need some time to let it sink in. I was so engrained in the teachings that I needed to lay my life down to follow God that the idea of God following a man took some getting used to, yet that's exactly what God told Joshua he would do.

This promise doesn't come in a vacuum, however. Just as I've talked some about the process God leads us through, there was a process Joshua went through before God made this promise to him. Joshua's training process included four important elements.

First, he learned what God desired from and in his life. This started right away when he heard God speak to the entire nation of Israel, proclaiming the Ten Commandments at Mount Sinai. It continued through the wilderness as God continued speaking to Israel through Moses, explaining layer upon layer of what he desired in their lives. As we see God told him in our passage, Joshua knew what God commanded. This established the foundation for his choices, ensuring that as long as he built his decisions on what God had already said, he would be building faithfully according to God's will.

Second, Joshua learned to trust and follow God during difficult times. More than once during the forty years in the wilderness, Joshua came face-to-face with people who wanted to kill him. He was the general who led Israel in battle, and at other times he stood before Israel as they cried out for his death so they could go back to Egypt.

Joshua knew very clearly that God gave him victory and help in times of trouble. While Joshua led Israel in battle in the valley, fighting for his life, Moses held his staff up in the air from the hilltop. When Moses lowered his arms, Israel began losing the battle, but when he raised them again they began winning again. In fact, when the battle was won, God told Moses to write what had happened in a scroll and make sure Joshua heard it (Exodus 17:8–16). Joshua knew his skill didn't change based on the position of Moses' arms, but that his victory came from God and God alone. He needed to know this as he entered the transitions of the Promised Land. He needed to know that his greatest need was God, keeping him humbly close to him and powerfully confident as he moved forward.

Third, Joshua cultivated relationship with God by meeting with him in intimate places. He did this by entering the tent of meeting with Moses and even staying behind after Moses left. He was present when God spoke to Moses face-to-face, when Moses had the encounters with God that made his face shine.

This shows he didn't just value God for what he would do for him. He wasn't just out for what he could get from God, but instead understood the value of God's presence and a relationship of faith with him. He walked in and practiced this for forty years, developing this value as a life habit. With this foundation, when God told Joshua he would go with him, you know that Joshua would go forth confidently but also would be continually turning his heart back to the Lord and his presence.

Fourth, Joshua discovered how to learn from spiritual fathers and mothers. He honored the generation that came before him in Moses, served him wholeheartedly, and remained faithful to him in the Lord. All that positioned him uniquely to inherit from Moses the role he now took up for Israel.

Consider this: If Joshua hadn't served Moses the way he did, who would have been in the right position to lead the nation? Of course God would have found someone else if he needed to, and he can always choose someone we wouldn't expect (and often does). Either way, the point is still that honor matters. There's a reason God's command to honor fathers and mothers is the only one with a promise—that if you honor your mother and father, it will go well with you and you will have a long life. Honoring past generations and truly receiving from them through honor really does invite blessings into our lives. Joshua learned this, applied it toward Moses, and reaped the blessings God promised.

This is quite a school Joshua went to. He learned to know God's will, to trust God all the time, to value his presence above all else, and to honor the authorities in his life. He learned them in the wilderness, and we will learn them too. As we do, they will take us to the same place they took him—a place where we can have confidence despite the risks we are called to take.

GOD ISN'T A CONTROL FREAK

When Joshua knew those four things, he was ready for God to tell him, "I'll follow you wherever you go." In essence, God had taught him the way he chose where to go. Once Joshua knew the wisdom God used in making decisions, he could reasonably make the same decisions God would make.

We see the disciples go through a similar graduation with Jesus as he spoke to them in the upper room before his crucifixion. Jesus told them, "No longer do I call you servants, for the servant does not know what his master is doing; but I have called you friends, for all that I have heard from my Father I have made known to you" (John 15:15). Even though Jesus had taught them with parables, he had explained many of them, and even though the disciples were still confused in many areas, Jesus still told them they had all they needed for a significant graduation.

Jesus had related to the disciples as his servants. He called them in the very beginning to follow him. Remember his famous words to Peter: "Come, follow me, and I will make you a fisher of men." The point in the beginning of their relationship was for them to follow him, but now he turns the tables on them. He lifts them out of the role of servant in their relationship with him and promotes them to friendship. He gives us only one reason for this promotion, that everything he'd heard from the Father he had passed on to them. There were no more secrets. Nothing was hidden. Everything was in the open.

No, it wasn't everything he wanted to tell them. It wasn't everything they needed for what they would soon be doing, leading a movement after he returned to heaven (the Holy Spirit would come to help them with that). But it was all the Father had given to him for that time. This is similar to the lessons Joshua learned.

Joshua knew the law of God; the disciples knew to love and serve one another. Joshua knew to trust God always; the disciples trusted Jesus enough to leave their lives to follow him. Joshua knew the value of God's presence; the disciples lived with Emmanuel—God with us. Joshua knew how to receive from spiritual and earthly authorities; the disciples had done just that for more than three years. All Jesus had from the Father, he passed on to them, and the understanding they gained from that revelation transformed them from slaves to friends.

Isn't it interesting that God led Joshua and the disciples to such similar places? He brought them all to a place where they knew him well enough that he could give them freedom. But we need to take one more step beyond just seeing that God did this to ask why he did this.

God brings us into this kind of freedom where he can honor our choices and follow us because he honestly isn't interested in controlling us. One of the fruits of the Spirit is self-control, and for a long time this confused me because I thought I was supposed to give God control of my life. Little did I understand that God never wanted to control me; he simply wanted me to lay down my misunderstandings about who he made me to be. To do that, I had to die to myself, lay down my plans for my life, and submit to a process in which he taught me his will for my life (my identity that directs my dominion), to trust him always, to value his presence above all, and to honor authorities in my life.

Through that, I learned that self-control is not God-control. I learned it's also not the same thing as gritting our teeth through a lifetime of struggles with sin. Instead, self-control is being free from all outside influence that has worked its way into our hearts—no bondage to sin, no wounds, no lies. In other words, it is freedom from those mindsets that tell us God isn't as good as he is and we aren't as amazing as he says we are. Self-control is being free to truly choose God out of love, not out of fear of hell or desperation for change in our lives.

CULTURES OF FRUITFULNESS

The message God shows us in how he treated those who drew near to him is a message of freedom for all who will simply draw near to him. But as I think of what it must have been like to be Joshua in that conversation, there's still one more question I need to answer: how did he learn to be brave instead of afraid?

It has to be more than simply that God commanded him to be brave. Believe me, when one of my children climbs into my bed at night and says, "I had a bad dream," it doesn't do any good for me to command them to stop being afraid. In that moment, they need something more powerful to come and displace their fear. This is the way fear works for every human. Fear can't just be shoed away; it has to be displaced.

To help answer this question, we'll return to a verse we looked at in a previous chapter, 1 John 4:18: "There is no fear in love, but perfect love casts out fear. For fear has to do with punishment, and whoever fears has not been perfected in love." It's interesting, but one element common to every controlling environment is fear, because control can only be maintained through fear of punishment. Control says, "You'd better do what I tell you to do or else!" The combination of someone's power to back up this threat and the corresponding person's fear of the threat is how a controlling environment begins.

Religious structures often use control. "Obey our laws or God will punish you." They become good at using Scripture to make it sound like their laws are God's laws, but they misunderstand the reason God gave the laws they quote. They don't understand God's heart to give us self-control rather than trying to control our lives himself. But think about how a controlling environment responds to a person's sins or mistakes—it responds with threats, fear, and shame in an effort to gain control.

Not far from where I live there's a conservatory that has several Bonsai trees. These are the carefully shaped miniature trees that look so beautiful. Once as I observed these trees, two things stood out to me. First, some of these tiny trees are over a hundred and fifty years old. It's incredible how such an old tree could remain so small. And second, I noticed that around several branches on each tree was a tightly coiled length of thick wire. It was wound in such a way that the tree had no choice about which way it would grow; it could only grow in the direction that had been predetermined for it.

All of these Bonsai trees are beautiful. They truly have become works of art, skillfully and patiently crafted through decades of intense control. They look amazing, but as art, they are not put in a place where they can reproduce. They will be beautifully controlled, but they will be alone. This is what our lives are like when we attempt to live by religious structures and laws in order to try to control our actions. Worse, it's the culture we try to force the world into when we tell them to be afraid of God's punishment if they don't shape up.

But what do you think a healthy opposite to the Bonsai tree might be? It's not a jungle, even though a jungle would truly be the opposite when it comes to freedom. While a Bonsai tree exists from sprout to death under extreme control, a jungle thrives in complete freedom. Yet while a jungle in the natural world serves necessary purposes, it's not what we want our lives to be like. That would be chaotic, messy, and overwhelming. We would have everything growing in our lives, both good and bad, and all of it would be bearing fruit. It's a double-minded existence where there's so much fruit of every kind that no one can tell who we serve.

The healthy opposite of a controlled Bonsai tree is an orchard. An orchard also has complete freedom, but our Keeper prunes what would limit fruitfulness so that we have fullness of life and maximum fruitfulness. As we remain in him, the Keeper also drives away everything that would shade us from his nourishing light and water.

This kind of freedom and fruitfulness come to those who have surrendered their identity to him (he'll tell you whether you're an apple, orange, almond, olive, or grapefruit tree), let the Lord plant them (going through the process like Joshua did), and allowed him to prune them for maximum fruitfulness (remaining in him because of love).

When Joshua entered the environment of God's love, it gave him freedom and courage to walk in who God made him to be. God promised to be faithful to him and simply asked Joshua to be faithful in return. Within that faithfulness, he didn't have to be afraid, because God would back up all Joshua's steps with his power to overcome every stronghold.

This is the relationship God wants to have with you. He created you to be strong and free. He made you to have a unique impact on this world that no one else can have. He made you to be just like him in a one-of-a-kind way. And he made you to be able to choose him, just as he chose you, because without that freedom to choose, something of his image would be missing in you. His goal is to lead you into his likeness, and his likeness includes freedom.

What are you going to do with your freedom? Start dreaming today by asking God who he made you to be. Let your being inform your doing. Commit to the process of growing into who you are. Remain in him; love well and serve well, not because of rules, but because that's who he is.

Then watch out, because you are going to change the world. And in case you need to hear it from someone, hear it from me—I believe in you.

NOTES

1. C. S. Lewis, *The Magician's Nephew*, (New York: HarperCollins, 1994) 127.
2. Brené Brown, "Listening to Shame," https://www.youtube.com/watch?v=psN1DORYYV0.
3. Wikipedia contributors, "Westminster Confession of Faith," *Wikipedia, The Free Encyclopedia*, August 26, 2016, https://en.wikipedia.org/wiki/Westminster_Confession_of_Faith.
4. Brené Brown, *The Gifts of Imperfection* (Center City, MN: Hazelden Publishing, 2010), 16–19.
5. There are many good resources out there to help you develop and keep good boundaries, but I highly recommend *Keep Your Love On* by Danny Silk.
6. "G1249 - diakonos - *Strong's Greek Lexicon* (KJV)," Blue Letter Bible, https://www.blueletterbible.org/lang/lexicon/lexicon.cfm?strongs=g1249.
7. "The history of Jesus Film Project," *Jesus Film Project*, http://www.jesusfilm.org/about/history.html.
8. Henry Ford, goodreads, https://www.goodreads.com/author/quotes/203714.Henry_Ford.
9. There are wonderful resources out there to help you declare God's words over your life. Some of my favorites include: Joel Osteen, *I Declare: 31 Promises to Speak Over Your Life;* Steve Backlund, *Let's Just Laugh at That,* David Crone, *Declarations that Empower Us* and *Victorious Mindsets.*
10. Kris Vallotton, *Moral Revolution*, (Ada, MI: Chosen Books, 2012), Apple iBook, 77–79.
11. "G3340 - metanoeō - *Strong's Greek Lexicon* (KJV)," *Blue Letter Bible*, https://www.blueletterbible.org/lang/lexicon/lexicon.cfm?Strongs=G3340&t=KJV.
12. "KJV Search Results for "kingdom" AND "of" AND "God"," *Blue Letter Bible*, https://www.blueletterbible.org//search/search.cfm?Criteria=kingdom+of+God&t=KJV#s=s_primary_0_1.
13. "KJV Search Results for "love"," *Blue Letter Bible*, https://www.blueletterbible.org//search/search.cfm?Criteria=love&t=KJV#s=s_primary_0_1.
14. "KJV Search Results for "grace"," *Blue Letter Bible*, https://www.blueletterbible.org//search/search.cfm?Criteria=grace&t=KJV#s=s_primary_0_1.
15. "KJV Search Results for "salvation"," *Blue Letter Bible*, https://www.blueletterbible.org//search/search.cfm?Criteria=salvation&t=KJV#s=s_primary_0_1.
16. Matt Damon and Robin Williams, *Good Will Hunting*, directed by Gus Van Sant (Santa Monica, CA: Lionsgate, 1998).